God, What Exactly Do You Want From Me?

from the author of **Desert Angel**...
Dorothy Aileen Dalton

God, What Exactly Do You Want From Me?
published by D. A. Dalton Publishers and Distributers, LLC
© 2006 by Dorothy Aileen Dalton

ISBN: 0-9766504-2-8
Printed in the United States of America

Most Scripture quotations are from:
The Holy Bible, New International Version ®
Copyright © 1973,1978, 1984 by International Bible Society
used by permission of Zondervan Publishing House

Also quoted:
The King James Version (KJV)

ALL RIGHTS RESERVED
No part of this publication may be reproduced, stored in a retrieval system, or transmitted, in any form or by any means, without prior written permission.

For information:
D.A. Dalton Publishers and Distributers
P.O. Box 115
Thompsonville, MI 49683

[1. Spiritual. 2. Family relationships. 3. Christian behavior. 4. Church relationships. 5. Spiritual Maturity.]

I would like to thank my fun-loving family Stephen, Andrew, Meredith, Mom, Dad, Judi, and Jamie for many of the stories used in this book.
Thanks to Doug, from The Church of Living God, for forcing us to find the answers!.
Thank you Lori, Ann, and Paul for painstakingly editing my work.
Thank you Andrea and Kathleen.
A special thank you to my husband for creating this idea, encouraging me to see it through, and for listening to me hour, after hour, after hour...

Contents

Introduction	Front Porch Sittin'	1
Chapter One	Meeting a Stranger	7
Chapter Two	Becoming A Child Again	17
Chapter Three	It's Right Under Your Nose!!!	23
Chapter Four	Afraid of the Dark	29
Chapter Five	"I'm Right Here!"	37
Chapter Six	What's On Your Mind?	41
Chapter Seven	What Are You Thankful For?	47
Chapter Eight	I Want My Daddy!!!	51
Chapter Nine	I Had A Really Bad Day!	59
Chapter Ten	Turn Off That TV!	69
Chapter Eleven	You Just Worry About You!	79
Chapter Twelve	You're Grounded!	89
Chapter Thirteen	Look at Me!	103
Chapter Fourteen	You Did All This For Me?	111
Chapter Fifteen	Is This Your Best?	117
Chapter Sixteen	You're Gonna Get It!	125
Chapter Seventeen	I'm Not Talking To You!	133
Chapter Eighteen	Who's Your Daddy?	141
Chapter Nineteen	Let's Go Over It Again!	147
Chapter Twenty	God, What Exactly Do You Want From Me?	157

Front Porch Sittin'

There are church people and there are those who aren't church people. I always wondered if some just went to church because they were hoping...that if they sang with the saints on Sunday morning maybe they would be forgiven for singing with the sinners on Saturday night! If they had a good heart, though, did it really matter? I didn't know.

As a child, I remember sitting on Grandma's humble front porch in the hills of West Virginia. Each evening, as the sun faded over the soft blue-gray mountains, we were serenaded by a family down the way. Their sagging, overcrowded front porch sported a banjo, a guitar, and some sweet voices harmonizing to the tunes of "What a friend we have in Jesus" and "The Old Rugged Cross." As we lazily listened to the faceless hillbillies, I remember thinking how those melodious voices, accompanied by Grandma's chicken and dumplings, created a place on this earth that couldn't be any closer to heaven.

One night, as all us barefoot cousins lounged on the lawn, I wondered....if you were really sincere when you whispered the words to "Amazing Grace," would it be enough faith to get you into heaven? If the words to "How Great Thou Art" could somehow fall upon the ears of Almighty God, would that be enough to meet Him one day? Would He even remember the night, during my childhood, when I hummed those old melodies with some good old country people of the faith? Would He remember what I was thinking and feeling on that night? Was He even up there at all?

My questions wandered and then finally rested on the front lawn. What if this was the last summer of my life that I would get to sit on Grandma's humble porch? Was this as close to God as I would ever get? Maybe it was impossible to get any closer! I didn't know.

I was able to spend a few more summers on that porch before I grew too old to visit the mountains. I've sat on many porches since then, however, and met many types of people with many different philosophies. Some times the new people in my life were confident that they knew what they believed and knew what they wanted. Others thought they knew what life was all about, but when a new philosophy became popular their "meaning of life" changed. Most of the time, people just talked to be talking. They were busy trying to convince others that their opinions were the best, while making a lot of excuses for why they didn't practice what they preached.

Front porch talk seldom gets more interesting than when someone brings up the topic of faith. I must admit, after thirty years of front porch sittin, I still don't have a whole lot of fancy, intellectual answers concerning faith. I've been swayed by family tradition to believe, by tragedy to not believe, and by experience to fall somewhere in between. Everyone I have met has battled with questions about church, about heaven, about Jesus...about God. I'm sure you, too, have worn the different shoes of doubt, disgust, and delusion, just as I have.

For a while, I didn't go to church because I didn't want to be around all those hypocrites and I definitely didn't want to go to a church where people ran up and down the aisle mumbling all that crazy stuff! I certainly was not going to let a bunch of finger-pointing, self-righteous people tell me what a loser-sinner I was and try to brainwash me! And all they wanted was money! I certainly wasn't going to pay them to put me down.

Sure I met a few that seemed genuine, but the majority seemed to exhaust themselves trying to outdo each other, trying to prove one was more religious than the next. It seemed to me that most of these church people were social outcasts suffering from low self esteem and they used the church as a crutch because they were too weak to deal with life.

Why would anyone want to continue hanging around a bunch of people that didn't even like themselves? It seemed as though their "great commission" was to find ways of making the *sinners* feel guilty, so they could make *themselves* feel better. I had wondered, if the church were truly comprised of God's people, then **why** would He allow them to act that way?

On my quest for spirituality I crossed paths with others that were interested in a "higher power." Some thought that there might be a God….somewhere out there…. but it was just too confusing, especially where heaven and hell were concerned. They couldn't make any sense of why a "loving and caring God" would send people to hell.

I was amazed to learn of those who assumed that if you are born in the United States, then you're automatically a Christian. And I thought the United States was founded on freedom of choice! Many in this group supposed that all good people go to heaven. As long as you do your best and your good outweighs your bad… then you had nothing to worry about. For those who needed to be a little more certain of their destiny, they secured their entrance into the pearly gates by attending a predetermined number of confessions or Sunday morning services. Some could have their family pray them into heaven when they died. Some felt they could do as they pleased because a large enough donation would ensure that St. Peter, himself, would show up and personally escort them into eternity. Still, others mindlessly followed family tradition. They believed the way they did because that's what they were taught, and if it was good enough for their great, great, great grandparents….then it was good enough for them! They were either too busy, or too complacent, to give their destiny any more thought. Believing what they were told would just have to do.

    I questioned prayer, for some time, simply because it seemed as though my prayers went unanswered. I didn't know how to get God to respond to me. Occasionally, it seemed like I would get what I prayed for, but it was rare. How am I suppose to trust someone that won't answer me? I reasoned, therefore, that God would only help when one really, *really*, **really** needs it!!! Keeping this in mind, I felt that asking too much of Him could nullify any request. In fact, I really didn't know how to get God's attention in a positive way, so I developed a fear of Him. I figured it best to exercise an "out of sight, out of mind" theory. If I didn't draw too much attention to myself, He might not strike me down with lightning every time I messed up.

Many people that I met throughout the years believed in Jesus, not really as the Son of God, but as a good example. He existed in order to create good moral bedtime stories for children. Many adults could recall going to church as a kid, but had decided that its value had since diminished.

An astonishing number of people had experienced some sort of Godly encounter. Some were even excited about serving God for a while, but then just got too busy, too distracted. Upon reflection, they weren't really sure if they were doing the whole "Christian" thing right anyway. They knew a lot about God, but they still felt like they had a lot of things mixed up. They felt like they were understanding the "church thing," but they didn't understand the "God thing." They weren't even sure if they were the same thing!!! They believed and loved Jesus, but still weren't sure if they belonged to Him. They didn't know, even after confessing their faith, if God was happy with them. They didn't know if they were saved from hell and despite how hard they tried, they *just didn't feel saved*. Many had no peace as they continually thought they were a disappointment to God. Many confessed believers didn't know exactly what to confess or exactly what to believe!!!

Others wanted to one day meet Jesus, but didn't believe Jesus could ever want to meet them. God's forgiveness could never catch up to their sin. All the tragedy in their lives and all the pain they had endured was because God had given up on them. Just like everyone else. They believed that they were lied to, beaten, used, and abused because they just didn't deserve any better. Some people were so crushed, so shattered, that they didn't know where to begin to look for help. They could only look down because they felt they weren't worthy enough to look up. They believed that they had made such a mess of their lives that not even God could straighten it out. They accepted that God must have been mad at them. They became so frustrated they questioned the existence of such an unforgiving deity, even though they knew differently. But the tugging at their heart, the nagging at their conscience wouldn't completely allow them to ignore God. The questions haunted them. What if I try to ignore God? What if I choose not to believe and I am wrong? What if I try, and I give it all I have, and I still fail? Why would God want me in the condition that I am in? It's too late. I have thought about it so much and I have felt so condemned, that I don't want to even think about it anymore! Deep inside me I feel like He's there, but it just doesn't make any sense. It's not logical. I'm so confused. Can't someone just make all this God stuff simple? Easy to understand? Can't someone just answer the simple question, **"God, what exactly do you want from me?"**

Meeting A Stranger

Chapter One

A few years back, I remember attending an employee Christmas party and being responsible for a present for someone that I didn't know. Few circumstances can be as uncomfortable as having to spend time with someone you barely know or having to search for a gift for someone that you have never met. Most of us have either been there or seen it happen to someone else. Maybe you bought a person a best-selling novel, only to find out they didn't like to read. Perhaps someone bought you a dried flower arrangement you were allergic to. How about those poor people that draw a name out of the hat like Sam. They confidently give him a gift card for a rugged, manly hunting store, only to find out that Sam was short for Samantha. Regardless of the situation, odds are that following the grueling selection process the gift is destined for the recipients' next yard sale anyway. This situation reminded me of a story about a new bride who married the man of her dreams…without meeting his family first:

> The holidays were just around the corner and the blissfully married couple was anticipating their first romantic Christmas together. The young newlyweds were so in love and never had life been so beautiful and satisfying. All of their hopes and dreams were met in each other's eyes and life could not have been any brighter or more promising.
>
> Because of their travels, they married abroad and the new bride was especially excited because she was going to meet her new in-laws for the first time. Because she could not do enough for her perfect husband, she gladly accepted the task of purchasing all the family Christmas presents. She lovingly went to her new husband for some suggestions. However, she received the ever helpful, typical husband response, "Oh honey, I'm sure they will love anything that you buy them." So, she appreciatively and adoringly kissed her husband goodbye as they each went to work.
>
> The window-shopping began. She constantly kept an eye open for that special gift from the two of them. She asked for advice from everyone she knew. Girlfriends, co-workers, family members, neighbors, and even strangers that looked like parents who might have a had a son who married someone before introducing her to them. The ideas swarmed in with mediocrity. However, the suggestions fell short of that special, sentimental gift that she was looking for. She peeked around every street corner, peered in countless windows, and followed the sound of Christmas music down endless store aisles. Thoughts of finding just the right present consumed her. Weeks of browsing, pushy salespeople, and specialty stores produced

nothing. The tree was decorated. Outdoor lights twinkled all over town. Even the neighborhood school children had been released for Christmas break. And still… no gift. She had not even found the perfect card or ideal wrapping paper.

Finally, the task had become too overwhelming. Frustration had arrived. As she discussed her situation with her friends at work, she found out how wise and seasoned in marriage they were. They offered her their complete support. They gave her a few lessons on the subject of marriage and how husbands are of little value and in-laws are uncaring thorns in your side. They educated her in how neglected and emotionally abused she had now become and the sooner she realized her little life was not her own, the better. She learned how she was now enslaved to a disrespectful family that will do nothing but tear her down for eternity. She lightly hyperventilated as her little innocent smile was replaced by a scowl and flared nostrils. She began wondering what kind of people would put her through such misery? My friends must be right, she thought. Only self-centered monsters would wish such agony upon her. Opinions and attitudes about the finicky, ungrateful in-laws escalated. Oh, she had met their type before! They're the type that are **never** satisfied! They're the kind that are sweet, until you leave the room, and then they secretly analyze you and recall all the good prospects their son could have married. Now that she thought about it, her conniving husband must be in on it, too. There was no use being nice to him anymore because he probably felt the same way they did. He hates me too, she thought. Why should I do anything for any of these people?

Finally, as she stormed through the mall she created a mental picture of the two scowling faces that probably posed for Norman Rockwell paintings. That's it! She made up her mind that these two evil relatives were not even worth her effort.

She didn't even feel the freezing December winds as she entered the cold dark night. This once sweet, considerate, meek girl flung open the door to the nearest restaurant and slammed her wallet on the counter of the popular steakhouse. With a gruff, demonic voice she bellowed, "Give me a gift certificate for two steak dinners!" She grudgingly paid for it and took herself and her attitude home.

The young obsessed girl grunted at her 'not-so-great-anymore' husband as he watched a woman, he did not know, storm into the house and throw everything she had on the floor. Her wet boots left little puddles as she marched to the desk, sending everything unwanted into a whirlwind. She rummaged through drawers until she finally found the box of old Christmas cards that she bought several years before because they were in a clearance bin......obviously because they weren't very attractive. She snatched the just purchased gift certificate from her coat pocket and into the card it went. She sealed the unsigned card in the envelope and coldly addressed it to "husband's parents" from their son and his wife. Let's face it, she just knew they didn't like her and her husband despised her so there was no need to be personal. She put the envelope back in her coat pocket and stomped off to bed.

Well, inevitably, morning arrived. Her cautious husband helped her pack and load the car. All she thought about, on the very quiet, eight-hour drive, was how her first Christmas with the love of her life had been ruined. Each time she felt that menacing card in her pocket it reminded her of shattered dreams. Candles, carols, pretty packages, and sweet kisses by twinkling lights. All of it gone never to return. All her holiday visions snuffed out, destroyed, and corrupted by these evil people and their vicious son.

Finally, her ungrateful, inhuman husband turned into the driveway and very carefully said, "well, Darling......we're here." Her lips tightened as he opened the car door for her. Her nostrils flared as they walked up the steps to knock on that perfectly painted door with that pretentious green and red wreath………………Only to be met **BY THE TWO SWEETEST, MOST BEAR-HUGGING, VEGETARIANS YOU COULD EVER MEET!!!** She just stood there in shock!!!. She stood frozen in time as these two precious little angels, sent straight from heaven, with kind smiles, and pleasant eyes, hugged her, kissed her, and genuinely welcomed her to their home. They went on, and on, and on, about how beautiful she was and how excited they were to have such a wonderful addition to their little family.

After the best home-cooked holiday meal one could imagine, the young bride still had that same silly, frozen look on her face. Next to a beautiful twinkling tree, the loving couple delicately put their precious new daughter-in-law in the seat of honor in the cozy living room. Not just any seat, but the seat that only Papa gets to sit in. Her husbands' mother festively announced that it was time to open presents. The young girl felt a lump in her throat as her caring husband retrieved her coat. With a sweaty palm, she reached into the cold, dark pocket and revealed the envelope. The envelope… of… destruction. She swallowed hard and closed her eyes as she put it in the hand of the sweet, delicate woman. Then she burst into tears and cried *out, "I'm sorry!" "I'm so sorry!" "I didn't know." "I just didn't know!"*

It is impossible to form a relationship with someone that we have never met. We can have all kinds of wild expectations and form unfair opinions of others that we know nothing about. Regardless of how the meeting occurs, an encounter of some sort is necessary. It's also necessary to spend some time with a person in order to know who they are, what their likes and dislikes are, and what they are all about. We have to be willing to give them a chance, to learn for ourselves about their character.

In addition, it's also unfair to make judgments based on the opinions of others. Getting an unbiased opinion from anyone is rather difficult. Many people are compelled to leave out or embellish information so others will see things their way. We have all had experiences in which we have heard terrible things about someone, only to meet them and discover they were nothing like what we had heard. Some of my best friends in life have been people that turned out to be nothing like I initially thought. Making decisions based on inaccurate information or what we dream up in our own heads is neither wise, nor fair.

It is the same with God. Just because someone goes to Sunday school as a child, does **not** mean they found God. Just because someone grows up in church, or a religious home, should **not** automatically suggest that they know how God thinks. The pious religious fanatic that you may work with, the one that points out the error of all your ways, does **not** reveal the nature of God. And your neighborhood hypocrite does **not** expose God's character. Most of these people are merely misinformed about God and they don't know what to do with what little information they do have. Simply, we cannot take the words, the actions, the preaching, or the teaching of anyone else and form an opinion about God. Each person, individually, must get to know Him and decide for him or herself. Decide who *He* is, what *He* thinks, what *He* expects, and what *He* is all about. God, Himself, even said in Hosea 4:6 that, "...my people are destroyed from lack of knowledge."

    I grew up in church, Sunday morning, Sunday night, Wednesday night, and everything in between. But like many, I developed many untruths about God. Some of my views reflected the opinions of others because I didn't take the time to investigate information. Other times, my views were based on ideas that I dreamed up in my own head because I was tired of not having any answers. I would easily accept the words of others as gospel, without comparing their words to His words. Like many people, the other views that I developed on my own were because I just didn't know any better. Nevertheless, it was, *and is*, my responsibility to research information for myself.

    Maybe you feel like I did. I had heard so many times that God was going to get me, that soon, He became an enemy.   An   enemy   is   anyone   or   anything   that opposes us.   The sermons I heard ended with a bolt of lightning coming down on my head as   God   thunderously   tracked   my   every   thought   and   movement. No matter how hard I tried each day, I was going to hell before I ever got out of bed. I watched the "saints" of the church preach love and argue over church decorations. I listened to "godly" people tell me that everything from TV to coffee was a sin, while they stumbled out of the town bar on Friday night. When I went to Christian College, my roommates secretly prayed for my deliverance because I listened to the radio. I gave up! I didn't even read the Bible because I figured it would probably explode when my impure hands touched it! I was baptized because it was the right thing to do and... because it was an evening of free swimming in a nice pool. Over and over, I remember hearing and thinking that the "man upstairs" was out to get me if I didn't do what was expected. Only I couldn't figure out exactly what was expected. It seemed, however, that I did have a lengthy list of "what-not-to-do's!"

Being around so much strife certainly didn't bring me any closer to God; in fact, it made me run. It made me run so far that, at times, I even questioned the existence of such a being. If God was this unfair and expected the impossible, then I really didn't want too much to do with Him or those employed in His church. Needless to say, although I had memorized a few key verses in the Bible and knew all the words to "Amazing Grace," I surely did not know God. He was a force, a higher power, that was just waiting for me to mess up bad enough to permanently get rid of me.

Upon becoming a parent, I thought my children should know about God, but I didn't want them having all the nightmares about Him as I did. Not knowing what to believe anymore, I decided to dabble in the world of church once again. We began listening to Christian radio and even found ourselves humming a few songs other than "Amazing Grace." I knew enough stories about Noah and Moses to teach Sunday school, so that worked out for a while. I even tried praying just because....you're supposed to.

Eventually, we wound up at a church that offered adult classes so we decided to try it. After all, we had been to a few potlucks and no bolts of lightning…yet! We could not believe what our instructor did! For every subject and every question, he made *us* look up the answers in the Bible. He hardly told us anything. We had to find the answers ourselves and then discuss it. What kind of philosophy is this, we wondered, not telling us how we should think or what we should believe? It was strange, but after careful consideration, we decided to stick it out for a while.

We had homework each week, and it led us through all kinds of books in the Bible. I was surprised at how many I still couldn't pronounce. I caught myself raising my hand in class with a question and then saying, "Oh, forget it! I'll look it up myself." Before long, I realized that the hard, rigid, unfair God that I had known, *wasn't even in the Bible**!!***   The Bible emphasized God's mercy, His love, His justice. When God *was* full of wrath, it was for one of several reasons. His anger was either aimed at those who mistreated His children, those who persistently disobeyed Him, or those that rejected Him. I found that when you do not see God's kindness, when you can't find His compassion then He appears to be a ruthless tyrant.

After this realization, I kept finding scripture after scripture on how much God loves us. How much He just wants a relationship with us. No matter how "good," or how "bad," I am, He is going to love me just the same. There is nothing my children could ever do that would make me stop loving them. And if God considers me His child, then there is nothing I can do to make Him stop loving me!!

Although I am now and then momentarily haunted by a lightning storm, (when I hear a crash of thunder I still yell toward heaven, "It wasn't ME!") I do understand that God is not trying to hunt me down. I now understand God's simple truth. In my marriage, God took a woman that had been running from Him for over thirty years and a man that didn't even want to mention God's name (unless he was mad) and gave them a gift of eternal life with Him, no matter how badly we mess up. The only thing I had to change was my mind. The rest of me, *He* changed. *Little* by *little*.

We must never let other people, lack of knowledge, or frustration force us into making unfair decisions concerning God. We must not allow others to manipulate us. How many times have we looked at our children and said, "God gave you a brain, so use it!" Well, the truth is, God gave us a brain, too--so we could use it! Ephesians 5:10 tells each of us to "...find out what pleases the Lord."

No matter what any of us believe, no matter whether or not we even believe in Jesus, the Bible clearly says in Philippians 2:10 and 11, "...at the name of Jesus every knee should bow, in heaven and on earth and under the earth, and every tongue confess that Jesus Christ is Lord." In this life, or the next, each person will have to come to terms with who the Lord is. Even Satan will one day have to confess that Jesus is Lord.

If we don't find out who God is for ourselves, if we don't spend some time trying to figure out what meaning life has, if we don't have an encounter with Jesus, then one day we will be like that young bride--in shock! We will look into the eyes of the Creator and with a frozen face we will be the one saying, "I'm sorry!" "I didn't know!" "I just didn't know!"

Becoming A Child Again
Chapter Two

When we bought our house we spent time researching where we wanted to live during the upcoming years. We certainly didn't want to live where we would be unhappy. So the way I figure it, if I have the right to choose where I'm going to spend eternity, then I'm going to research that destination as well. After all, it's my life, and forever is too long to spend it where I don't want to be. It's too long to be unhappy! It's bad enough being at the Department of Motor Vehicles for too long. And if that is any indication of what hell is like, then this decision deserves my attention. And I'm the one that will be doing the investigating. We would never have bought our home based solely on information we had obtained from someone else. Some would have thought it was great and others would have thought it wasn't. We had to investigate the property for ourselves. This was our dwelling and we were the only ones that could make that decision. And eternity is a dwelling, a place that goes on and on, forever...and ever...and ever...and ever. I am not going to allow anyone, whether they are pro-God or anti-God, to persuade me in making this decision either. I am the only one that can make it. My parents can't make it for me. My friends can't make it for me. Even my husband can't make it for me. This one is between me and God. Just God. Not between me and a priest. Not between me and a Bible teacher. Not between me and someone knocking at my door with good intentions. Sure they can present me with information, but the decision is all mine. No one can share in this quest. This one is all about me!! And I am done....completely done....with being confused!!

All through the Bible God continually refers to those that love Him as His children. And He understands children. He wants His children to do their best, but understands that we can get things pretty mixed up. He knows that the thinking of children can get a little crazy. That's why He looks into their hearts. I wonder...if God ever looks down at the earth, the way parents sometimes look down at their kids, and says, "Yeah, they may be brats, but they're my brats!"

Love and truth are God's most important teachings. God knows that we will not understand everything, but He does want His children to be faithful to what they do understand. He just wants them to be real.

In Mark 10:15 we find that Jesus was indignant with His disciples for the way they were treating others. He goes on to say, "I tell you the truth, anyone who will not receive the kingdom of God like a little child will never enter it." Notice, He was upset with His own people, His very own disciples. His chosen ones! It doesn't say that He struck them with lightning, caned them, or even condemned them. He corrected them with a verbal and visual example. He then took all the children in his arms and blessed them. He showed us all that God has compassion and mercy for His children.

Matthew 18:3 and 4 is another example of many scriptures that say, "I tell you the truth, unless you change and become like little children, you will never enter the kingdom of heaven. Therefore, whoever humbles himself like this child is the greatest in the kingdom of heaven." Only those who are like children will spend eternity with God. I'm 41 and I still don't know what I want to be when I grow up. My husband refuses to grow up, so this really works for us. We must realize, however, Jesus is not directing us to be immature. He's simply encouraging us to be innocent and pure in heart. To realize that He is God and we are not. To erase our minds of all preconceived religious ideas, so we can innocently look to God as our Father and simply understand that those who love Him are His children.

Realizing that God viewed those who loved Him as His children allowed me to understand Him and what He expected from me. My husband and I started looking at our children and wondering if they were a reflection of God's children. As we began to study them, we started asking questions. What if God were trying to say the same things to us that we say to our children? What if we do the same things to God that our children do to us? Does God look at us as we look at them, with the same emotion, discipline, and commitment? We realized that we could learn a lot about God from our children. Our children and God's children have much in common. In many ways, we act just like they do. In Mark 9, the disciples were walking down the road arguing over which one of them Jesus liked better! Even the chosen twelve of Jesus acted like children. Just as we do not expect our children to perform the impossible, God does not expect His children to perform the impossible. Just as we expect our children to behave, God expects the same from His children. Just as we expect our children to experience, learn, and grow, God expects the same for us. Just as our children mimic us, God expects us to mimic Him.

When we consider how many times that Jesus refers to the humble innocence of children and the number of times God refers to those that love Him as His children, then we must conclude that having the heart of a child is essential. If the Bible is calling us to be like children, then God would have to expect us to understand, **and misunderstand,** as children do. For example, look at Jesus' chosen twelve. He was continually taking them aside, redirecting their attention, and explaining things they didn't understand. I think He put that group in "time out" more than I ever did my children.

It's pretty interesting, and humorous, to compare our children to God's children. But if we do, we can better understand *why* we do what we do and *why* God does what God does.

All of us have had doubts and questions just like those porch sittin' people in the beginning. Whether you happen to be one that is not sure if you believe in God, or one that believes but doesn't know where to go from there, or a seasoned believer that just has a few things mixed up, we all need to look up at God with the eyes of an innocent child. For some of us, we need to look up at God the same way our children look at someone they have never met. We need to look up at the Lord, introduce ourselves, and begin a new relationship. We need to pretend we have never heard of Him, we have never met Him, and just start over! Some will need to shake His hand and meet Him for the first time. Unless children are taught differently, they are trusting, honest, and real--everything God calls His children to be. Like them, with an open and accepting heart, we need to get to know God the way He really is. We need to study and accept what is true and throw out what is false. He already knows all about us and now it is our turn to find out all about Him.

    I believe God calls all believers His children, because He expects us to enjoy the wonderful world that He created through the heart and through the eyes of a child. He expects us to live, and love, with the enthusiastic heart of a child. He expects us to look at Him, our Father, with the passionate and adoring eyes of a child.

    This is what my children have taught me about being one of God's children.

It's Right Under Your Nose!!!
Chapter Three

    Anyone with older children knows that it is physically impossible for them to find anything on their own. It's astounding how many times a day we are asked, "Mom, where's my mittens?" "Have you seen my math book?" "Where's my other tennis shoe?" "Where do you keep the glue?" Our responses to these thoughtless questions are nothing more than catchy retorts like, "Where did you see it last?" "Right where it always is," and "In the same spot you left it!"

    The "I can't find anything" drama, if nothing else, sure is entertaining. My son couldn't find the remote control one day. I watched that child walk in circles for all of five seconds, grunting as he turned over the same pillow three times, then drag his burdened little feet to the couch, and fall face first in exhaustion! The climax of the performance was when he wearily looked up at me, with puppy dog eyes, and breathlessly moaned, "I tried....I really tried....but I just....couldn't....find it!" After the child breathed his last, I peered over my glasses, walked over to the coffee table, picked up the remote, put it in his lifeless little hand, and said, "It was right under your nose."

He picked his head up and said, "Oh!"

Shortly after this award winning production, my teenage son was in hot pursuit of his blue knit cap. "Where's my blue hat?" he shouted as he thundered into the living room.

"In the closet, right where it always is," was my reply to the monotonous question. That boy swung open the closet door, looked straight in front of him, shut the door just as fast as he opened it, and screamed, ***"I CAN'T FIND IT!!"***

In disbelief, I stomped over to the closet, nudged him out of the way, and without even looking, opened the door, reached for the shelf, and retrieved his hat. In astonishment, I said, "Son, it was right under your nose!"

He looked at me, then down at the hat, then back up at me, and said, "Oh!"

My first response was, "What do they expect me to do?" "Do they want me to walk around making their little lives perfect, doing whatever they don't want to do, going behind them fixing everything they mess up?" Secondly, I thought maybe I could organize things better. I could try to make things easier for them. So I organized. I got baskets for this and containers for that. I hung new shelves. I grouped things. I labeled things. I classified things. I arranged things. They all watched, in boredom, as I gave lessons on how organized things should be kept. But...IT WAS ALL IN VAIN! It didn't make any difference; they still couldn't find anything. In defeat, I whimpered, "I can't make it any easier, it's right under your nose!"

I soon realized that I had misdiagnosed the ailment. The problem wasn't that their lives were too difficult, because making things simpler sure wasn't the cure. The problem was that they were either too lazy, or too busy, to figure things out for themselves.

The straw that broke the camel's back came a little later. My son sat at the table working on some homework when I heard him complaining, "I just don't get it!" As he sat with his head in his hands, he cried out, "Mom, this is too hard, I just don't get it!"

Sympathetically I sat down beside him and looked over the assignment, "Well, Buddy, what did the directions say?"

He gave me a perplexed look and said, "I don't know, I didn't read them."

With the same perplexed look that he had given me, I replied, "How do you expect to do anything, if you don't read the directions?"

He just said, "Oh!"

I felt a "mommy fit" rising up in me and decided that it would be best for all if I retreated to another part of the house. In frustration, I put my hands on my hips, huffed my way back to the kitchen and began putting away the dishes. You know, the loud way. The way that the clanging and banging can be heard for several country miles. And because I'm trying to be more spiritual these days, I decided to take my complaints to God:

"Now I know they are just children and they have reached the age where hormones have robbed their little brains of any normal activity, but they are struggling with ridiculous things. If they would just do their part, then they wouldn't have so many issues. I mean, it's obvious that you need to read the directions in order to do something new. It's pretty clear that with a little

effort, life would be a lot less difficult. If they would only listen to me when I'm trying to communicate something, they could avoid a lot of stress. If they weren't so lazy, then they would realize that the answers to their problems are right under their nose. Can I possibly make it any easier?"

I felt my "mommy fit" being interrupted by God's response:

> *"I know just how you feel. I'm right here where I have always been waiting to communicate with all my children, but*
> *do you know how few will stop long enough to talk with me? People say, 'Oh, I tried praying once, but nothing happened.' What they mean is they didn't get what they wanted, so they dismissed the idea of God.*
>
> *I gave everyone my beautiful creations from the awesome creatures of the deep seas to the highest peaks of my majestic mountains; from the great canyons and breathtaking waterfalls to the stars of the wondrous galaxies above. And they still doubt my existence.*
>
> *I gave my people the Church so they could help each other, but it takes too much effort to get up on Sunday mornings. Talk about excuses, people avoid my church for more reasons than you could ever imagine. All just excuses.*
>
> *Tell me about reading directions, I left a whole bunch of them in that book I wrote. You know, the dusty one on the shelf that you call the Bible. Most think that*

its sole purpose is to keep an accurate account of their family tree. For those who do go to church, it's the same book that they leave at home because it's too heavy or it doesn't match their outfit. Many people will open the Bible, flip through the pages for all of five seconds, drop it on the bed and whimper in defeat, 'I just couldn't find anything!' Some will make a commitment to read it everyday, but it only lasts for about a week.

What do they expect from Me? Do they want me to go around making their little lives perfect, to do whatever they don't want to do, to go behind them fixing everything they mess up?

Do you know how many times people go to some 'spiritual' person for advice instead of seeking me? It's so much easier to have someone tell them what the right thing to do is, rather than finding out for themselves. It's much more entertaining to turn on a popular therapist in the afternoon and hear what they have to say, than it is to read my teachings to find out what I have to say. Then they get mad when they get bad advice.

And you wouldn't BELIEVE the number of stressed people that fall face first on their couches, crying miserably, calling out for some understanding, wanting answers for all of the problems they caused in the first place because they didn't obey the directions I had written for them.

Now I know you are all just children and life can be very confusing which can rob you of determination, but there are so many struggles you would not have if you would just do your part and seek Me. When you enter your adult life, it's obvious you are going to need to read the instructions and as I already said, I made a very complete booklet. I even organized it, gave examples, and put much of it in story form so you could understand it. Yet some people don't even try to "get it" and others get too religious to "get it." I mean, you should see the number of Christians that hardly ever read the directions. They tell everyone what's right and what's wrong, and what they should and shouldn't do, and they don't know anything about me. No wonder many of my churches are a mess.

It's pretty clear that life would be a lot simpler if people would just pay attention. If they would just look up at me and allow me to direct them. It's evident that with a little effort life would be a lot less difficult. If you would listen when I'm trying to communicate something, then you would avoid a lot of stress. EVERY answer to EVERY problem, EVERYTHING you will EVER need to know to live in joy and to live in peace in this world... is in My Bible. I cannot make it any easier. It's right under your nose!"

I just said, "Oh!"

Afraid Of The Dark
Chapter Four

Many children have a monster or two in their heads, perhaps a boogieman under the bed or a hairy three-eyed creature in the closet. Regardless of the monster, most of us can remember waking up in a sweat because of a childhood nightmare.

When our children are young fears are based on their imaginations. Things they create in their minds. When the nightmares begin they want us to peek under their beds, but all we find are a few forgotten toys and missing socks. When they ask us to check the closet, we open the door and make a similar announcement…"Nothing alive and child-consuming in there, either!" We take a few minutes to hold their hand and reassure them that everything is all right. "I love you, I'm not going to let anything happen to you," we repeat as we slowly back out of the room. "I'll leave the light on." "I'm right here, right down the hall." "Remember God's watching us, too and God **never**, **ever** goes to sleep!"

However, night after night the light stays on as they lie in wait for the monsters. They listen to every household creak and stair squeak. They rarely miss a tree branch rubbing against the house. Until one night, when they decide that they don't believe in that stuff anymore. One night they will make the decision that their faith is bigger than the monsters.

As they grow, however, imaginary fear is later replaced with fear of the unknown. These fears begin to emerge as they realize the monsters aren't just in their heads anymore. They are the real things in the world that are potential problems. These monsters are the bad things that can happen to them. It can mean sleepless nights worrying about falling off their bikes, public embarrassment, rejection, harm coming to their family, and death. Older children don't normally get our attention with screams, but they still want us to hold their hands and talk to them. Our reassurances include, "I love you," "I'm going to look after you," and "We taught you to avoid wrong influences and situations." "It probably will hurt if you fall off your bike or if someone is mean to you, but we will be here to ease the pain and encourage you to try again. It's the only way you are going to learn." "People are going to die, but if they know Jesus, then they are leaving this world to go to a perfect existence." " We teach you all that we do and want you to follow our rules only because we want you to be both safe and prepared for the world." "You know God is always watching, He promises to be our ultimate protector." We finally add, as we leave the light on, "and just because you are older, does not mean God goes to sleep."

One night, an hour after I initially went to bed, I found myself resting beside a frightened preschooler and a snoring husband.   While I tried to sleep on the remaining six inches of bed left to me, I couldn't help thinking of what incredible imaginations my children have! How do they think up all this stuff? How much sleep have I lost because they dream up situations that have never happened and never will happen?   I wonder……….. how much sleep I have lost because *I've* worried about a lot of stuff that was never going to happen either? How many monsters do *I* have under my bed? How many disturbing creatures are in *my* pantry closet?

When we think about it, we realize that adults have monsters that chase them around in the night, too. Adult monsters come in the form of fear, dread, worry, and negative thinking. Fear is a monster that keeps us up at night. Dread is a monster that keeps us from enjoying life. Worry is a monster that robs us of peace of mind and quality time with others. Negative thinking is a monster that prevents you from pursuing your dreams. These are all monsters that rear their ugly heads when we hit the pillow at the end of the day. We fear harm that can come to our children, especially when they start school, begin driving, or leave home.   We dread going to work because something didn't go well the day before.   We worry about money, the economy, climbing unemployment rates and the inability to care for our families.   These worries can cause us to question our faith.   Is God really bigger than the interest rate?   Is God really going to take care of us if I loose my job? Is God paying attention at all?

Negative thinking usually hits me when I'm cooking or washing dishes. It's the monster that dominates our thoughts with ridiculous, irrelevant situations that have never happened and probably never will. This includes all the scenarios that go through our heads, for hours at a time, about possible confrontations. What we are going to do if this person does this and what we are going to say if this person says that? It's thinking about a situation that happened seven years ago and how we are just waiting for the right time to let that person have it. It's the big "what if" game. We all play it. What if there is a terrorist on my airplane, and the pilot passes out from a rare altitude condition, and I have to single handedly land the plane? What if I win the lottery, how am I going to explain to the church where the money came from? What if I run into my husbands' ex-girlfriend from third grade and she's skinnier than I am?

Negative thinking is just like the imaginary monsters our little ones have under their beds. It's stuff we make up and that ridiculously consumes our thoughts. All these monsters lurk in the darkness. We hear the creaks of financial ruin and the squeaks of jealously that can destroy relationships. We can hear the harmless tree branches that rub against the house and believe that it's destruction and death that have shown up for someone we love. Like our kids, we see shadows, too. But our shadows can be shadows of despair, depression, and blind fear. Despair, if left unchecked, can devour our whole lives and leave us believing that there is nothing to wake up for in the morning. Depression consumes decades that could have been spent enjoying our work, our play, and the people we love. Fear can cause total blindness, a darkness so thick that we can't see the closest person to us...not even God. The only difference between us and our children is, the bigger we get... the bigger the MONSTERS! No three-eyed monster has ever eaten a four year old in the middle of the night, but the monsters of depression and despair have surely eaten many adults in the dark of the night. The green monster of jealously has killed many, many marriages. And the monster of insecurity has murdered millions of dreams.

What monsters do you face? Which monsters have you cornered? What ones have messed up your head, kept you from thinking clearly, from making rational decisions? What monsters are lying to you, telling you that you are worthless and your dreams will never come true? That you can never be a good enough parent! Which ones are telling you that no one will ever want you around, not even God? What monsters are lying to you, telling you that you need to trade in your God-given life of peace for a life of worry?

When our children's fears manifest, we need to find out what generated them. Maybe it was a bad movie they saw, or a scary story they heard. Things they have seen or heard can haunt them for years. Our own cares and worries are fed the same way. If we are surrounded by negative people, then what they say will have a negative effect on us. Think back to the last time you worked with, or spent the day with, someone that said *nothing* positive. Everything that came out of their mouth was mean-spirited, critical, or caused some sort of strife. By the end of the day, your own thoughts were also negative and it was difficult to find good in anything.

Satan takes every chance that he can and seizes every opportunity to jump into our heads. Every time we allow something negative in, Satan comes along for a free ride and magnifies the problem. That's why we can take the smallest of situations and, in no time, turn them into something huge. One morning we can have a sore throat and a little cough and by early afternoon we believe ourselves to be suffering from a life-threatening, incurable, untreatable illness that researchers haven't even discovered yet. It sounds crazy, but many, many, many people magnify their problems and then wonder why they live under so much stress. When we look at fear, worry, and stress closely, we see that there is a lot of truth to this "making mountains out of molehills" mentality. If someone becomes upset, Satan begins to feed them emotionally and their state of mind can lead to a discouraging day and a sleepless night. A series of discouraging days and sleepless nights may lead to weeks of depression and a sleep disorder. Months of depression and sleep disorders can lead to eating disorders and immune system problems. Before you know it, high blood pressure, heart problems, and blood diseases have arrived. Finally, these conditions may lead to a heart attack or a stroke, resulting in death. Then someone asks what the person died from and our answer is, "Oh... they were just upset." Obviously, as we seek to rid our children of fear and stress, we need to be just as concerned with these emotions in our own lives.

God gave us our imaginations so we could create and dream. So we could imagine ourselves in those dreams, and with God's guidance, we would be encouraged to achieve them. However Satan came along and introduced our imaginations to fear and terror. Consequently, imaginations that were designed for creating dreams, began creating nightmares.

Our children have a choice to make when we leave their bedrooms each night. The choice to believe that we are looking after them, and that God is in control, or the choice to stay in that little room terrified, without hope. God, as He always does, creates a way out for us, too. We have a choice. God is always providing us with choices. We may live in the anxiety and terror of the nightmare or exercise the faith in Christ that offers us the peace and tranquility of the dream. Our kids have to make the choice and we have to make the choice. Is their faith bigger than the monster? Is ours?

Just as we want our children to call to us for help, God wants His children to call upon Him for help. We can even scream for help if we need to! When our children are afraid of the dark, we turn on the light for them. When we are afraid of the dark, God turns on the light for us. Being a believer in Jesus does **not** mean that the monsters do not come. It does **not** mean that we can't feel overwhelmed by negativity and darkness. It does **not** mean that we are never lonely, desperate, stressed, angry, or terrified. It does **not** mean that we never go to any of these places. *It means…that we don't have to stay there!* Our children are going to become scared, but they don't have to stay scared! We are going to walk into negativity, but we don't have to become negative ourselves! God calls this deliverance. If we decide to exercise the option of calling on our Heavenly Father, then He will *always, always, always,* turn on the light. And when that light comes on, when we open up the Book of Truth, we hear God's soothing, most comforting voice as He walks with us along the path of peace. In 1 Peter 5:7 God says, "Cast all your anxiety on Him because He cares for you." Psalm 76:7 says, "You alone are to be feared." (respected) Psalm 73:23 states, "…you hold me by my right hand." Psalm 73:26 says, "My flesh and my heart may fail, but God is the strength of my heart and my portion forever." Matthew 6:27, "Who of you by worrying can add a single hour to his life?" Psalm 23:4, "Even though I walk through the valley of the shadow of death, I will fear no evil, for you are with me;" And Jesus said in John 8:12, "I am the light of the world. Whoever follows me will never walk in darkness, but will have the light of life."

Outside of our souls, the greatest gift we can ever give to Satan is our mind. The biggest playground that he has, is the playground in our mind. When we start worrying, fearing, dreading, and thinking negatively, we invite him over to play. And he loves a good game of fear and a couple rounds of worry. So, if you don't want to play with the monsters, or play in the dark, remember...God is waiting for you. Waiting for you to ask Him, to turn on the light. He's saying,

"Just hold My hand, I've got you, and I love you. I am not going to let anything happen to you. I've taught you that everything you need to know is in My Word, so you would know how to deal with all the problems and insecurities you will face. Oh, I know it will hurt when others mistreat you, but I am here to ease the pain and encourage you to try again. I am always watching. I'm your ultimate protector. You are not alone. And remember! Just because you are older, does not mean I go to sleep!!"

"I'm Right Here!"
Chapter Five

There are some things that God never meant for us to outgrow. Some of our characteristics should remain as simple and pure, as when we were children. When my children were small, I can remember repeating phrases over…and over…and over. Repetition and consistency is how they learned. As they grew, however, I didn't need to repeat new lessons as often for them to grasp the new concept. They developed a means of figuring things out for themselves. And that is what we want for them, to figure, to problem solve, to stand on their own two feet.

There is, however, one phrase that I still repeat often… "I'm right here!" When they were babies and they needed me, they would cry and I would pick them up and say, "I'm right here!" When they would fall and get hurt, I would come running, "I'm right here!" When other children wouldn't play nicely, they would come crying to the back door and I would open it and say, "I'm right here!"

Just because they are older their need to call out to me in their distress hasn't changed. And although their activities sure have changed, my response hasn't. When they are out of money, they call out from the porch and I reach for my wallet saying, "I'm right here!" They call after running their car into a ditch, and I answer and say, "I'm right here!" When they are disappointed because they weren't selected, or they were treated unfairly, I make them a special snack and say, "I'm right here!" When their grandfather died and they bitterly sobbed the afternoon away, I handed them tissue after tissue saying, "I'm right here!"

I am so glad they *want* me when they need something. I am so glad they feel *comfortable* enough, and *trust* me enough, to come to me. I am so glad they *love* me enough to come to me. And I am so glad they know that I love them enough, any time...day or night... to say, "I'm right here!"

None of them have left home yet, so I don't know how often they will need someone to say those words in the future. I know I left home a long time ago, though, and I sure need to hear them. In fact, I need to hear those words a lot!

I'm so thankful that I, too, have a parent that is always available. God always wants us to bring our concerns to Him and He is always faithful. Never too busy. Never too distracted.

God gave us our children to raise, protect, instruct, love, and be the ones to tell, "I'm right here." By the time they become adults, however, the Lord expects us to have taught them to call on Him, whenever they need to hear those words.

When we believe in the wonderful mercy of God and

the endless love of Jesus, we are given the right to call on Him any time of day or night. It doesn't matter when or what we're doing. It doesn't matter if we're at work, mowing the lawn, or just can't sleep. As with a parent, there is no bad time to call on Him.

When we get hurt God is saying, "I'm right here!" When others don't play nice, when we are mistreated, He will say, "I'm right here!" When we are out of money or lacking anything, when we wreck our car, our marriage, or anything else, He's saying, "I'm right here!" When tragedy strikes and you feel like crying many afternoons away, He will always say, ***"I'M RIGHT HERE!!"***

We will never outgrow needing a Father to be there unconditionally. No one can outgrow God! He is so glad you **want** Him, when you need something. He wants you to be **comfortable** enough, to come to Him. He wants you to **trust** Him enough, to come to Him. He wants you to **love** Him enough, to come to Him. And He wants you to know that He loves you enough, any time…day or night…to say, "I'm right here!"

What's On Your Mind?
Chapter Six

After our first child was born, we wanted to do the "right thing" and teach him to say his prayers before bed. We ceremonially knelt beside the bed with bowed heads, folded hands, and closed eyes. Then we began the "Now I lay me down to sleep, I pray the Lord my soul to keep…" prayer.

One night, my little one looked up at me and said, "Why do I have to say this poem and who is this Lord Guy anyway?"

I was kind of shocked by the question and responded the same way all good parents do when asked a question they don't know the answer to, "We'll talk about it in the morning," I said.

When I addressed the question the following morning, my response was typical. I let him know that the Lord is God and God is way up in the sky, in a place we call Heaven. Saying our prayers, or "heavenly poems," is talking to God.

"Well, if I'm going to talk to God, shouldn't I say what

I'm thinking?" he asked.

"That makes sense," I quickly agreed, "say whatever's on your mind!"

As I sipped my morning coffee I realized, I did the same thing! I had this little ritual prayer that I recited before I went to bed, each night.

Dear God,
Please watch over my family and keep us all safe and healthy. Amen

That was it. It was spiritual procedure to quote the same thing every night. Like a poem without rhythm. This wasn't talking to God. I only said this nightly prayer to satisfy my own spiritual requirements. If I "said my prayers" I would be in good standing with God. My superstition was strong enough that I felt it necessary to wave around some predetermined words in order to keep evil away. It was kind of like…don't walk under a ladder…don't break a mirror…and don't forget to say your prayers!

Although I considered myself somewhat "spiritually challenged" at this time, I knew that prayer was something God expected. I started thinking about other times that I prayed. We would pray before we ate. Well, at least at Thanksgiving and Christmas. Well… only if Grandma or some other religious person was present. I prayed if I was going to a job interview. Oh!.....I also prayed before I had surgery or if someone in my family was really sick!

I decided that I really did want to give God a chance in my life, but the last thing I wanted was to be religious. I just wanted it to be simple. I didn't lack the desire to live for God. I didn't lack the faith to believe in Jesus. I didn't even lack the devotion to be close to the Holy Spirit. I simply lacked understanding. I didn't want the process of getting to know God to be some big mystery that had to be solved. Do this...no don't do that! This is acceptable...no it's not! God's mad at me...no God loves me! I should read the Bible, but not that version! Be passionate, but emotion is a sin! Help the sinner, but don't go near him!

     I have learned that no matter how much I read the Bible or listen to sermons, it will not change my life if I don't have understanding. If I don't have understanding, then I will never fully believe. And if I never believe, then *I can't live the life God wants me to live*!! If I am going to pursue God, then He needs to be more than just a concept that is too big for me to understand. Jesus needs to be more than just a historical figure that pioneered a new philosophy called the "Golden Rule." My son was right! Prayer is talking to God and we should say whatever is on our minds. We know that beginning a relationship with someone requires talking to them and taking time to know them. Praying is taking time to know God. No more cute rhythmic prayers or neatly arranged words that rhyme. No more talking to God just to satisfy my own definition of spirituality….or….to avoid seven years bad luck.

     I was very serious when I said I wanted to do this "God thing" without confusion. So I started doing the two most important things that one can do. I began reading God's Word **and** praying. Reading and praying!! I am sure that Satan was upset because this combination was lethal. I was killing his plans. I gained understanding. I began to comprehend what a wonderful life God had planned for me. I started believing God's Word. The character of God starting showing through me, not because of anything great I had done, but because God **promised** He would pour out as much truth, understanding, and wisdom as we could handle. My life was becoming more and more blessed because I began wanting God more than anything else. When we make God first, He doesn't just **send** blessings, He **pours** blessings on us. I made God's words first in my life, not the words of others. I learned from studying the New Testament that Jesus was not impressed by fancy rhyming words and public displays of religious prayer.

To make it even more simple, prayer is our response to God's question, "What's on your mind?" Fully and sincerely discussing our thoughts, joys, and concerns with God. I know...God knows what we are thinking, but He wants to hear us say it. My husband knows I love him, but he still likes to hear me say it.

The Bible tells us that prayer is power. Through *prayer* we receive power to overcome adversity. Through *prayer* we receive power to become victorious over our enemies. Through *prayer* we receive power to overcome opposition in our lives. Through *prayer*, we receive power to extend our arms of faith, far enough to reach our dreams.

In Mark, chapter nine, the disciples were unable to heal a boy. They tried, but it didn't work. The people were curious why the power of Jesus didn't seem to be enough. The problem was that the disciples had not prayed enough and that's why the miracle didn't happen. The power had to be fueled by prayer. Jesus often removed himself from the public in order to pray.   *Prayer* is the fuel that we need to live beyond mediocrity. *Prayer* is the fuel we need to achieve our destiny. *Prayer* is the fuel we need to reach our dreams. *Prayer* is the fuel that changes our lives and the lives of others.

Pray before you even get out of bed!   In Psalm 5:3 we read, "In the morning, O Lord, you hear my voice; in the morning I lay my requests before you and wait in expectation." Proverbs 16:3 says, "Commit to the Lord whatever you do, and your plans will succeed."   King David is saying that because he prayed before his day got started, because he put the Lord before all else, because all that he thought and did was dedicated to the Lord, **God would answer him!. Anything, anything, anything that he did, God would bless!!!**   Because David wanted God's will in his life, David could pray **expecting** an answer any moment. He was confident that God would make him prosper in every way.   If God is foremost in our lives, we can pray expecting an answer any moment. We can be confident that God will prosper us in every way, also.   If we commit our efforts to God, meaning that we want the same things that God wants, then we can jump out of bed in the morning knowing and expecting God to show up on our behalf. Each day He will show up, just like He did for David.

A decision to love God and follow Him is what will get us from this earth to heaven. But a decision to earnestly pray, will bring heaven on earth.

If you don't know what to pray about, then just imagine God asking you, "What's on your mind?" If it matters to us, then it matters to Him.   He wants us to tell Him about our relationships, the good ones and the bad ones. He wants us to tell Him about our families, the joyful moments and the disappointing moments. He even wants us to tell Him when our husbands are being insensitive and when our wives nag too much! He wants us to ask for help concerning our weaknesses, our challenges, our failures, and our fears. He wants us to thank Him for our joys, our strengths, and our victories. Matthew 7:11 tells us that God wants to give His children good gifts. Therefore, He wants us to tell Him about our desires and our dreams. If we want to go anywhere with God, then we have to understand that God finds us important! His children are the most significant of all His creations and He is concerned with the most intimate details of our lives. We are so valuable to Him that He is not willing to be separated from any of us for a single moment.

There is no special uniform to wear when we pray, no designated way to hold our hands or our heads. No arranged way to stand, bow, or kneel. It's just a personal conversation between us and God. We can pray with others or alone. The only way prayer is wrong is when we are not being sincere or when we do it to impress others.

Just talk to Jesus throughout your day. Whenever you think of it. Whenever you need Him. Prayer is sharing the details of our lives with our Heavenly Father. He finds us so interesting that He tells us in the Bible to pray without ceasing. He wants the lines of communication open so we can continually talk to Him. As we work, as we play, as we drive, as we shop, as we fish, as we change the oil in the truck... whatever we do. We are so important to Him, that every moment of our day, God is asking, "What's on your mind?"

What Are You Thankful For?
Chapter Seven

     Today is what my family considers the second best holiday of the year, Thanksgiving. Next to the Christmas season, this holiday can't be beat. Each of the children submit a list of their edible requests, weeks in advance, and begin drooling over the turkey while it's still frozen. In our family, we believe in emphasizing the things that we do well and one of the things that we do best is......eat. And we practice with enthusiasm!!!

     On Thanksgiving morning, the children sit at the counter inhaling the aroma of fresh baked apple pie and staring at the oven. They take turns asking, "How much longer?" about every half hour. I take this opportunity, each year, to ask the same question that most of you do, "What are you thankful for?" You have to love Thanksgiving, because their responses are not like those during the Christmas season. At the top of their list is their family, then a warm home, the dog, and, of course, good food! Their responses are basic and sincere, emphasizing what they love and cherish most, the relationship we have with each other and being together. Sure they know we give them all the other things, but on this one day they aren't looking to see what we can get for them, do for them, or where we can take them. They are looking into our faces with gratitude, not looking into our hands for a twenty. This is a day they appreciate us for just being there, for unconditionally loving them, for providing for them, and for being constant and reliable. It is so nice to be appreciated!

In Deuteronomy, the Israelites were promised by God to be blessed, and continually blessed, if they remembered where all their blessings came from. If they forgot and took the credit for themselves, then the blessings would cease. He was telling them that, like us, He wanted to be appreciated. Giving thanks was a very serious part of God's relationship with His people. God even expects us to open our prayers with thanksgiving. In Psalm 100 verse 4 we read, "Enter his gates with thanksgiving and his courts with praise;"

It was that way then and is still that way now. We don't want our children being spoiled and ungrateful and God doesn't want His children to be spoiled and ungrateful, either. Although we give our children wonderful gifts and material things, we want them to appreciate the giver, not just the gift. And although God gives His children wonderful gifts and material things, He wants them to appreciate the Giver and not just the gift.

We need to remember and recognize God for all that we have, all that we are able to do, and all that we will ever be. We need to just sit in awe that He is the best thing that has ever happened to us. He very simply wants to be at the top of our list. A list that is basic and sincere, emphasizing what we love and cherish most, the relationship we have with each other and being together.   He wants to know that we are not always seeking stuff, what He can get for us, do for us, or where He can take us.   That's why Jesus said in Matthew 6:33,   "But seek first his kingdom and his righteousness, and all these things will be given to you as well."   We need to look into His face with gratitude and not always look into His hand for a gift. It's appreciating Him for just being there, for unconditionally loving us, for providing for us, and for being constant and reliable. Then God is given the opportunity to look down from heaven, at His children, and say, "It is so nice to be appreciated!"

I Want My Daddy!!!
Chapter Eight

First, you hear the stampede of little feet. Next, comes the crash! Finally, the scream!! Quickly, you run to the scene of the accident and check for blood and broken bones. Although the wailing and screaming would suggest that they just cheated death and are mere moments from needing life saving surgery, most of the time it's nothing more than a bump or a skinned knee. "I WANT MY DADDYYYYY!!!!!" they cry. When my kids are upset, only their father can adequately calm them. When they are scared, their father is the only comfort they will accept. They know that if he's there, then everything will be all right. Quite simply, when life presents its problems, only their father will do.

Most of the time when my children get hurt it's because they are doing something that we have told them, *over and over*, not to do because we knew someone was going to get hurt. They think we make rules just to be mean and in control. Nevertheless, we still don't want to see our children in pain. We want to take away the sting and wipe their tears.

Sometimes, we have to sit on the sidelines and watch, knowing our children are going to get hurt. As they learn to ride a bike, we know we had better have some bandages on hand. As they become interested in sports, it can lead to pulled muscles, torn ligaments, and more. When they begin dating, we cringe at the thought of their hearts being broken. Although we know that all these aches and pains are part of growing, we still feel for them.

At other times, the little ones we care about can be hurt by careless or malicious people. We spend a lot of time educating them on how to avoid such circumstances. We drill them about not talking to strangers, choosing the right friends, and steering clear of immoral and dangerous environments. We try to train them and protect them because we know that someday they will have to make such choices for themselves.

No matter how we wish that they could go through life without grief or pain, occasionally they are going to get hurt. As parents, we want to come to their rescue. As friends, we want to comfort others when their world falls apart. As a husband, you want to protect your wife. And especially as a Christian, we just want to fix everything. We feel a strong inclination to help others, to try to fix what's wrong in the lives of the people we know and love. All are natural tendencies and are noble efforts.

I can think of times in my adult life that I have looked up to Heaven in distress, wondering how things could have gone so wrong and wondering why they had to happen to me. Feeling so hurt and helpless. Wondering if God was even watching, let alone was He concerned. If He was truly there, why didn't He fix everything? I wanted Him to make it all go away. I wanted Him to just make me stop hurting.

God knows that His children are also going to get hurt. Although He told us *over and over*, in the Bible, not to do what we were doing because He knew we were going to get hurt, He still doesn't want to see us in pain. You see, God's children often think He makes up rules just because He's mean and wants to be in control. But He knew we were going to crash and burn, just as our children do. And He feels just the way we do. In our grief, He picks us up and takes away the sting through His forgiveness.

Sometimes our Father has to sit on the sidelines and watch, knowing that we are going to get hurt. In order to become who He created us to be, we must learn and grow. The trials we go through build our character. The battles we win make us stronger. The tests we pass make us wiser. God cringes at the thought of our hearts being broken. Although He knows that all these aches and pains are part of growing, He still feels for us.

God also knows that there are a lot of nasty people out there. He knows that Satan, in all his power, wants to destroy us. He wants to spend a lot of time educating us, through His Word, on how to avoid these evil circumstances. He drills us about staying away from wicked people, choosing the right influences, and steering clear of immorality. He wants to train us and protect us so that when we are confronted with evil, we will make the right choices.

What happens when we stand in the way of our children's growth? We can protect them so much that they never learn that fire is hot, that not going to school leads to illiteracy, and that dishonesty breeds a lack of integrity. Like earthly parents, if God didn't allow His children the chance to learn, then they would ultimately suffer.

    To be a Christian person is to be Christ-like in character, in mind, in heart, in behavior, and in attitude. Simply to be like Jesus. In the Bible we see that Jesus encountered a lot of hurting, mistreated, and misguided people. But we don't see Jesus running after them. They came to Him. They were drawn to His kindness, His love, and His peace. And He did more than just put a band-aid on their wounds. For all who wanted it, He healed them inside and out. He healed them everywhere they hurt. But most importantly, Jesus pointed them toward Himself and God. He taught that all they needed was Him. He did not direct them toward well-meaning people with lots of advice.

    Our list of doing good for others, in the name of God, should be ongoing and sincere. It is just as important to want to help others, as it is to actually do the work. If we just go through the motions, then it is not having a heart like Jesus. Don't you hate it when someone offers assistance of some kind and you know they didn't really mean it, they were just trying to be polite? What about when people insist on helping and you don't want their help, because it actually creates more work? You wish that they would have let you come to them.

    A difficult, but vital, lesson that we need to learn is when to run to the rescue and when to sit on the sidelines. Remember, Jesus didn't run to anyone. They came to Him. Unfortunately, everyone I know suffers from accumulating problems, such as broken homes, shattered dreams, or unfulfilled desires of some sort. At one time or another, we all experience a family crisis. It could be unemployment, an illness, or death. That's the way life is and as my husband always says, "whoever told you that life was going to be perfect, lied!"

Let's take a minute to remember, from scripture, why painful things happen. They may happen because a person has made a bad choice, intentional or unintentional. Many times bad things happen because God is trying to get someone's attention. Perhaps that person doesn't believe in Him. Perhaps they believe that Jesus existed, but that the Bible is just a bunch of moral bedtime stories. Perhaps someone has more faith in a church, or a particular belief system then they do the One True God. Maybe they know God, but aren't obeying Him. Or perhaps they believe in Him, but they don't have much to do with Him; they just aren't as close to Him as they once were.

Just as we want to be close to our children, God wants to be close to us. Just as we want to be part of their lives and enjoy them, God wants to be part of our lives and enjoy us. Through the good and the bad. When our children go through their little lives ignoring us and disregarding what we have taught them, then we take them aside and remind them. In order to gain their attention, sometimes only a gentle reminder is needed and other times our methods of discipline need to be a little stronger. We were created to walk **with** God and when we go through life barely considering our relationship with Him, then He is going to try to gain our attention.

It is so easy to try and help others with their problems,

especially if they are someone we really love, but often we end up being a hindrance or a distraction. Surely, we can cook dinner for a sick friend. God calls us to encourage those who are down-hearted. We should give to those that are less fortunate. But all these acts are just "band-aids." They help people while they are healing. But we can not pretend that we are the healer. We can not let people assume that we are the problem solvers. We can not allow people to mistake us for their deliverer. We can not permit people to think that we can always protect them. And we can not make people think that we are always right and they should always follow our direction. Like Jesus, all that we do needs to point to Him and God. If we are always in someone's face trying to tell them what they should do and how they should do it, then they are not going to see Jesus. Because we are blocking their view, they will see only us. When they have a bad day, they'll call us, not Him. When they're mistreated, they will want us to make it right, not Him. When they're having financial problems they'll look to us and not Him. They can't see the hand of God, or the face of Jesus, when we are standing in their way.

This reminds me of when I was young and we would play in front of the TV, my Dad would say, "Move, I can't see through you!" Sometimes God is saying, "Move, they can't see through you!" Every single person needs to learn and see for themselves that God is their answer. Not us "all-knowing" Christians. Not a therapist. Not a friend. Not a husband or wife. Not even a mother or father. Because we all know that there are days when none of these are going to be available. God, on the other hand, is *always* available.

Everyone needs to know, for themselves, that our Heavenly Father is the *One* that will hold their hand and that Jesus is the *One* who really has the perfect solutions. The One who really is their salvation and their deliverer. The *One* who really is their comforter, their protector, and their vindicator. The *One* who really is their healer and their miracle worker. We can offer a shoulder to cry on, but, remember, we can only cover the wound, we can not heal it! We need to kindly point them toward heaven and release them from our care and place them directly into the hands of The Father, into His care.

When we crash and burn, just like our children, we need to cry out, "I want my DADDY!" Whether it be a little crisis or a big crisis, whether the problem be in the heat of the afternoon or in the middle of the cold, dark night, we are God's children and it is O.K. to call out to Him. In fact, He expects us to. When we are upset we need to understand that it is our Heavenly Father that can truly calm us. When we are scared then our Father is the comfort that we should seek. We need to know that as long as He's in control, then everything will be alright. Quite simply, when life presents it's problems….*only* our Father will do!

I Had A Really Bad Day!!
Chapter Nine

Occasionally, one of our children will walk in the door with an unmistakable look of defeat. "What's wrong?," I cautiously inquire.

"**EVERYTHING**!" he snaps, "**I HAD A REALLY, REALLY BAD DAY**!!"

I make him a favorite snack as he describes the series of little mishaps that ruined the day. Nothing went right. First, he was late getting to class because he lost his lunch money on the playground. Then he couldn't find his math homework and the teacher was mad. He was supposed to return a comic book to a friend, but forgot, and now his best friend in the whole wide world doesn't want to be best friends in the whole wide world, anymore. The series of unfortunate events worsens as he recalls an unforgettable bus ride home, featuring a bully and mobs of laughing children. "I couldn't do anything right! I don't want to be me anymore! I just want today to go away!" he whimpers in defeat.

Compared to our adult world their little trials may seem insignificant, but to them it's a very big deal. That night, as we tucked their overwhelmed little selves into bed, we promise that tomorrow would be a much better day. We encourage them by letting them know they are not alone. We all had days like this. It's part of growing up. As parents, we still feel sorry for them because they are so distraught they can't even see any reason to get up tomorrow.

The wonderful thing about children is their resilience. Somehow, during the night their little minds completely erase the day before. They are capable of deleting the entire days' disasters from their memories. They get up, jump on the bed, throw some toys around the room, and they are ready to embrace another day. There are baseballs to be thrown today, bikes to ride, snakes to catch, and huge handfuls of popcorn to shove into their mouths....when Mom isn't looking, of course. It's amazing! They can be ready to throw in the towel, but after a good night sleep, are ready to flick someone on the behind with the same towel!

Why is it, when we grow up, we loose one of the most valuable assets we could ever possess? Namely, the ability to forgive and forget. The ability to pout for a while, then take a shot of enthusiasm, and be healed from the trivial annoyances in life. With a hug, or a cookie, or a cartoon, troubles seem to just disappear.

I believe Jesus uses children as examples, so often, because they are so humble and forgiving. He encourages us to recognize and latch on to their sincerity and innocence. God wants us to unconditionally love and forgive as they do. He wants us to be zealous about Him and what we care about. To discover passion for all things and people that we hold close. But we tend to give up our youthful enthusiasm and become serious, overbearing, Prozac-popping, control freaks.

Think back to the last time you had a bad day. Maybe even today. When you didn't hear the alarm in the morning, had no clean underwear in the drawer, and every telemarketer in the country randomly reached your number. You forgot to take the garbage out and it was already oozing out the sides, you forgot your Mother's birthday, and she had already left you three voice mails wondering where she went wrong raising you. So you run to the store and the only gifts you can find scream "last minute!" I guess that's what you get for trying to birthday shop at a convenience store. You stand in line ten minutes to check out, only to remember you are out of coffee, so you grab it and have to go back to the end of the line again because they only have *ONE* employee! You get home to find a note from your husband, pleading with you to not to forget his dish to pass for the office party that started an hour ago, **AND THERE IS NO CHOCOLATE IN THE HOUSE, ANYWHERE!!!!!**

That's it!! You have officially reached the end. You have nothing left. You can't take anymore. You cry, "God, just take me away," as you slump into the recliner. You would pray, but you don't know what to say or where to start. You have been completely robbed, not only of your joy, but your energy as well.

That old Satan is nothing but a great big bully. The more frustrated we become, the bigger, meaner, and more intimidating he becomes. John 10:10 tells us that Satan comes to steal, kill, and destroy (paraphrased). If you are a Christian, he can't take your soul, but he will try to rob you of everything else. What better way for him to get us out of his way, then to make us feel beat up, abused, and unappreciated. He does his best to push our beat-up selves into a an old recliner, as often as possible. If he had his way, we would never get up out of that chair; we would stay there feeling depressed, hopeless, and abandoned.

When we're at the point when we are done, we're without joy, which the Bible says is our strength, then we can't even muster up the initiative to talk to anyone, not...even...God! When we don't enjoy anyone, or anything, we tend to withdraw. That's what Satan wants us to do! When we are not close to God, we are left open and vulnerable, and that means our protection is gone. Then one bad day, turns into a bad week. A bad week into a bad month. And there are some people that are on bad decades. Can you imagine how miserable it would be to be sick and tired, frustrated, fed-up, depressed, hateful, and numb for a decade?

Remember, Satan is nothing but a bully. What do we tell our children to do with bullies? We don't give in to them and one way or another they will go away. That really is in the Bible. In the book of James 4:7 and 8 we find these words, "Submit yourselves, then, to God. Resist the devil, and he will flee from you. Come near to God and he will come near to you." That simply means, turn your attention to God. Take your eyes off the devil and your circumstances. Begin focusing on the provision instead of the problem. Satan may be the problem causer, but God is our problem solver. In other words, don't pay the devil any attention, don't believe him, and don't give him a reason to pick on you. The Bible tells us that he then will go away.

If we are doing things that we know we shouldn't, then that gives Satan the right to capitalize on our sin. Like we said before, it is an open invitation for him to come over and play with our minds, our situations, and our lives. When we make a bad choice, Satan will capitalize on our mistake and make an even bigger deal out of it. He'll rub guilt in our faces and make us think that there is no remedy and no forgiveness. If we drop God as our defense by stepping onto Satan's territory, then Satan can come at us and we have nothing to protect us. You see, Satan can suck the joy right out of us. Then we are no good to ourselves, let alone anyone else. If he's really done a good job on us, we don't even have the energy, or the will, to call out to God. That's the plan of a bully. To corner us. Alone. No one to watch our backs. By obeying God's Word, we secure a protective barrier around us that the enemy can't penetrate. It's when we choose to not follow His instructions, to not obey Him, or to not walk humbly before Him with a genuine love for others, that those walls crumble. He promises that the righteous are never forsaken. The many accounts in the Bible prove the same truth over and over. The only times that the righteous are not delivered are when they disobey Him or it is their time to be taken to heaven with Him. God decided the day each one of us would take our first breath and He will also decide the day we take our last.

Jesus warned us that we would have bad days. He guaranteed it in the scriptures. At times he referred to them as trials and He said **when** they come, not if they come. If being a believer in God meant we would all prance around on a puffy little cloud with perfect hair, then wouldn't everyone become a believer? If being a believer meant that you could snap your fingers and, like a genie, could produce a rustic fishing lodge with endless trophy bass, people would be flocking to church. That may be the way it will be in heaven, but, on earth, we are told that Satan will pursue us. And if Satan is hot after you, then Psalms 145:18 says, "The Lord is near to all who call on him, to all who call on him in truth." God has compassion for all He has made and when we call on Him, He will catch us when we fall. When we tumble into that old recliner, fed up with responsibility, disappointed in relationships, weakened by illness, longing for some peace and quiet, that fall is so soft because we land right in the arms of the Lord.

It is O.K. to become discouraged. It's O.K. to become frustrated and fed-up. It's O.K. to realize our limitations. And it is O.K. to be human. We need to understand that it is not a sin to have a bad day. The sin is in staying there or pretending to be too good, too godly, and too perfect for it to happen to us. The sin is playing "super Christian" that goes to "super church" as we leap over adversity in a single bound. The sin is pretending we are faster at finding all the spiritual answers than a speeding bullet. Only God can do that. Unfortunately, this is why many unbelievers label Christians as "hypocrites" because they know that no matter how religious one may try so very hard to be, a "super Christian" can not live up to all that they profess to be.

    It's time for the church to just be real. It's not practical, or even godly, to pretend that everything in our lives is perfect. This is one reason why many people don't want to come to church; they feel as if their lives don't measure up. And the last thing a new-comer wants, is to be just another hypocrite sitting in a pew on Sunday morning. Sometimes our behavior, even if we have the best intentions, can make people run **from** Jesus, instead of **to** Him. It's unfortunate that we can make others feel as if they need to get their lives in order *before* they try to get with God because they fail to realize, that God is the very One that gets our lives in order for us.

    We all know there are everyday trials we must deal with and we have to be diligent in dealing with them. Just like our children, we can have a conflict with one person and we feel like everyone hates us. We can mess up one or two things and we feel like we can't do anything right. Circumstances can so overwhelm us, at times, that if we don't take the time to recognize the problems for what they are, they will turn into really big problems. Then it will take more than just one night to restore us. It will take a long time, sometimes even a life time, to repair the damage of denial and playing the role of the self-proclaimed martyr.

It is godly to take time out to restore our souls. God frequently refers to restoration in the Bible. Jesus said in Matthew 11:29 and 30 "Take my yoke upon you and learn from me, for I am gentle and humble in heart, and you will find rest for your souls. For my yoke is easy and my burden is light." Jesus knew restoration was necessary for those occasional bad days.

Let's take our frustrations to God. When we don't want to be us, hand everything over to God. When we feel so distraught we can't even see any reason to get up tomorrow, give it to Jesus. Let's give Him all of our problems. Just lay them at the feet of the Great Comforter and take a few steps back...relax...and let Him restore us.

Ladies, grab those old baggy, flannel pajamas (the ones your husband hates), some chocolate, a bag of chips, your Bible, and thank God for some time alone. Men, grab a fishing pole or your hiking shoes and head to the great outdoors, or wherever your sanctuary is, and thank God for some time to spend with Him. It's during our escape, that God restores our soul and strengthens us for another day. If we don't take the time out to give Him our soul, then He can't restore it. If we don't take the time to give Him our broken, worn-out spirit, then He can't heal it. We are given free will and He does **not** wrestle us for our time, He'll only repair what we ask Him to. James 4:2 says, "You do not have, because you do not ask God."

Compared to God's world, His "Big Picture," our little trials, like the trials of our children, seem insignificant.

But we have to remember that God looks at us in the same way we look at our children. He feels sorry that we go through what we do, but He knows that it is part of "growing up." He knew, since the beginning of time, there would be bad days and that's why He put all those uplifting scriptures in His book, to encourage us. Psalm 30:5 says, "...weeping may remain for a night, but rejoicing comes in the morning." It is His promise to us, as He tucks us in at night, that if we center our lives around Him, tomorrow will be a much better day.

Let's try to be more like our children. During the night, let's allow God to restore us. To erase our minds of the previous day. Let's allow Him to delete the disasters of the day from our memory. To remind us that we are His children, and as His children, we may not be perfect, but we're getting closer. We may not know everything, but we're learning. We may not have all the answers, but we have more than we did before. We may not fearlessly face everything, but at least we aren't running. We may still make mistakes, but we don't make as many. We may not always be right, but we're not wrong nearly as often. As God encourages us to remember that we are His children, heirs to His throne, and brothers with Christ, we will awaken refreshed standing strong as overcomers, conquerors, and warriors. And after all this encouragement, support, and restoration.....let's get up in the morning and throw off those covers with enthusiasm. I don't even believe that it's a sin to jump on the bed a few times! Let's forgive and forget. Let all the weight Satan is trying to put on our shoulders go, and embrace a beautiful gift that God has given.....a brand new day!!! Let's flick our spouse with a towel and thankfully shove a fistful of popcorn in our mouths... even if people are looking!

Turn Off That Tv!
Chapter Ten

Most parents can sympathize with this dilemma. Every moment my children can break away that little button on the TV goes on. If it's not the TV, then it's a video game. If it's not a video game, then it's the computer and its abundance of gaming choices. Rarely would they choose to do anything else. Creative activites, physical activities, conversation, family interaction, and good old fashioned play are just shy of extinction. We all know how unhealthy this is. We certainly preach it enough in our house.

It had gotten to the point that we couldn't even assemble for a meal together. A flash in the kitchen would indicate that an adolescent body was close by and with a disappearing plate, a vanishing glass, and a "Thanks Mom," everyone dispersed back to their personal caves of electronics.

We had roller blades we never used, bikes we never

rode. River property we never enjoyed. Skis that never left the garage, and we live less than three miles from a resort! We didn't play with the dog, build forts, dig holes, get dirty, or go fishing. In fact, it became an enormous effort just to do the grocery shopping so we had junk food to munch on, while we sat in front of the TV. We didn't read stories together, make up stories together, or go to the library. I couldn't remember the last time I had the camera out to take pictures of anyone because no one had moved from in front of a screen, since last Christmas when they opended up their new DVD's and computer games!

    One day I yelled, "that's it! TURN OFF THAT TV!" It was time that we addressed these issues and we decided that this behavior had to stop! We were amazed at how totally useless everyone had become. They didn't even want to leave the house to go have fun. I would offer a day at the mall or the beach, but they preferred a movie that they had already seen eight times. They knew the dialogue so well that they could recite the lines and never miss a word. They were spending their lives watching other people live theirs! The distraction was so intense we barely spent any time together as a family.

    Following the "Electronics Address," my husband and I retreated to our room with our dinner plates, grabbed the remote, and began surfing for our usual entertainment.

    "Can you believe those children?" my husband remarked, "what a waste of their little existence."

    "Life is going to pass them right by!" I mindlessly added.

    We like hockey in our house and games are usually on

two or three nights a week. On the other nights we had our favorite shows that we liked to watch. However, **we** were responsible, during the commericals we found the time to run the dishwasher, throw in a load of laundry, and straighten up for the morning.

As I went to sleep that night, I prayed for our poor little lazy children. "God, help them to see that there is so much more to life than TV."

Immediately my eyes flew open and I gasped at what went through my mind. "Surely, God, you are not implying that we do the same thing. Come on now. The house is clean, the laundry folded, the yard mowed, the checking account balanced. We really enjoy the things that we watch and it's totally different." I exorcised this ridiculous thought from my head. Maybe I just ate too much pizza before bed and it's making me think crazy.

Our little talk the night before was effective because the next morning, our little angels showed up at the breakfast table right on time, dressed and ready to start their day. I was impressed. It usually takes more than one speech to get them to respond this well. The only one that wasn't there on time... was me. The only television on... was mine, but I needed to catch the weather and the news before my day officially started. They patiently waited for me to arrive at the table with their food.

We were supposed to enjoy some time together, reading, before the days activities began, but I had to postpone the story now because I was a bit behind. "We'll read at lunch time," I stalled.

Following lunch, a friend called that I hadn't spoken

with in some time. That conversation lasted better than an hour and so I postponed our "reading time" again. I was so tired, by this time, because the hockey game had gone into double overtime and I needed a cat nap so I could make it the rest of the day. I justified a nap because I did manage to clean out a closet and organize our bills during commercials and in between my home improvement shows. Oh, and I did catch two TV preachers on in the morning so I did get some religious instruction.

After a quick two hour nap, I felt a little better, but I needed a shower and some coffee to wake up completely and get things ready for our family dinner.

Dinner was on the table in a timely manner and after arguing about where everyone was to sit, we prayed and started our meal with family conversation. *Our new resolutions were coming along quite nicely*, I thought. Well... at least until the phone rang and I had to be excused for the rest of the meal because it was someone that really needed some advice.

We decided that after dinner everyone could have a little television time because they had been so good that day and it gave Dad some time to unwind and me some time to call my sister and my mother.

I finished my telephone calls in time to quickly tuck the kids in and make it for one of our shows. It was a rerun, but it was really a good episode. Besides wholesome viewing is good for us. I need time to relax, too.

Well, another day had ended and I began my prayers.

Thank you, God, for your help with changing our children and their bad habits. You are so faithful to help us become the best that we can be. Amen.

I was ready for a good night sleep once again. Well deserved, I might add.

After a few minutes passed, I sighed, "Not again!" unaware that I had spoken out loud.

"What?" my husband mumbled.

"I keep getting this feeling that I am no better than the children about this whole "distraction" thing, I said. In my defense, I explained all that I had accomplished throughout the day, including a freshly mopped kitchen floor and a grocery list made up for the next day's shopping. "Why do I feel so defeated? Why do I feel that I wasn't as productive as I should have been? Why do I feel as if I didn't manage my time well?"

"Don't be silly, honey, you are not one of the kids. This is about them, not about us," he managed.

I was unable to sleep as I recalled the events of the day. I'm sure my insomnia had nothing to do with a two hour nap, either. Was it my faulth that it was the day my favorite television shows were on? You know how it is, you miss one and you are all messed up. Was it my fault that friends needed my help, today? Was it my fault that I was tired?

The answers were yes, Yes, and YES!!! It was my fault. I calculated, in my head, how much time I had actually spent talking with my husband and sharing quality time with him. The results.....Not even twenty minutes out of the entire day! The time I had spent with my children, directly, wasn't much better. Less than forty-five minutes! And time with God? Well, if you don't count the two TV *preachers that I sort of listened to while I did other things.....None. I felt awful. My own plan had failed because of Me! I was so distracted that I put everything before God, my children, and my husband.*

Those feelings were not my own imagination, guilt, or pizza. Those feelings were subtle messages from the Almighty One, Himself. He was trying to convey the same idea to me, as I was to my children. And He didn't stop with just my priority issues at home. We had attended church regularly, well...when we had time and could get up in the morning. But we were pretty faithful attending Wednesday night classes...if we weren't too tired and it wasn't during the play-offs.

We figured everything was all right because we had been taught that God does not condemn us! He loves us and accepts us just the way we are! That is very true, but that doesn't mean that He allows us to sit idle and waste the short time that we have on this earth. God doesn't want to condemn me, but He does send moments of conviction. Those are His gentle words that encourage me to live more. Live better. Always wanting me to take the "high road." Condemning words and attitudes tear people down, but words of conviction cause us to examine ourselves and look for ways to continually improve who we are. They are constructive words that help us be the best that we can be. God was simply trying to tell me,

I made a big beautiful world for you and blessed you with such a wonderful fun family, now get up and

enjoy it!! I want more time with you each day. More than just half-heartedly listening to some TV evangelists and a two-line prayer before you go to sleep. I want you to grow by spending some time in MY Word each day. Even if it's for just a few minutes, as long as it's a sincere few minutes of your best, not your leftovers. I have great things to tell you, but you are so busy listening to your girlfriends, that I can't get a word in edgewise. Quit trying to fix the world, that's My job!

Oh, and that handsome husband I gave you, he definitely deserves more attention than you are giving that phone. Everyone you talk to on the phone, knows more about your life and who you are than he does. And those beautiful children. It's about time you create some memories. Get out the camcorder, the camera, and make some unforgettable days. In fact, make everyday unforgettable.

Of course, major improvements didn't happen over night. It was a long process because there were a lot of areas in our lives that needed "renovating." We had to practice balancing our commitments and play time. We had to diminish the time spent on some activities and cut out certain ones altogether.

With all this in mind, I now read God's Word almost every morning before my day even begins. There are many verses in the Bible about laziness. Proverbs 12:24 says, "Diligent hands will rule, but laziness ends in slave labor." Provers 10:4 says, "Lazy hands make a man poor, but diligent hands bring wealth."

I just "happened" to be reading Proverbs when I was going through this little dilemma. God is amazing. When we are going through hard times or when He's trying to teach us something. He always leads us to the scriptures that we need to read. I guess, that is what He means by tryng to share His thoughts with us. When He has something to say to us, it will somehow be right in front of us. We just have to open the Book or open our eyes and ears.

I think that most people that have opened a Bible in their lives have experienced this. God will sometimes speak to us through what we are reading. I am always in awe, when I turn on Christian radio or television and the discussion of the day is amazinly familiar to my little crisis or situation. I love it when we go to church and the lesson of the week answers the questions that have been on my mind. This is no mistake. God is just that perfect and God wants to communicate with us, just that much.

To avoid distractions, we need to address them first thing in the morning. Scripture tells us, often, that we should go to God before we do anything else. I like to read and pray after my husband goes to work and before I get the kids up. I know my husband enjoys time with the Lord on his ride into work or on his boat while fishing. God made us different, so it stands to reason that we would communicate with Him differently. It is vital to our existence because distractions can be some of our worst enemies. Distractions keep us from overcoming challenges, from conquering tough issues, from accomplishing our goals, and reaching our destiny. We are all created with greatness in mind. God does not want any of us, including our children, to settle for a life of mediocrity. We are children of the Most High God and we should know that God wants to give us His best. We should go to bed each night satisfied that today was lived to the fullest, and wake up each morning ready to embrace a new day that is even better than the day before. The Bible tells us that each day we should expect God to meet us, walk with us, open doors for us, and escort us into blessing that we will not be able to contain! If we stay focused on Him, on His love, on His purpose, then He will give us all the desires of our heart. The Bible really does say that and often.

    If your dreams are not coming true, if life is less than satisfying, if you feel like something is missing, if you have even a faint feeling that you were created for more, if you are tired of just being tired... then maybe you have too many distractions. Maybe you need to get alone with God! Maybe you need to turn off that TV!

You Just Worry About You!
Chapter Eleven

Today was a "play day" and each one of the kids had a friend over for the afternoon. It had been a calm morning and everyone worked together to finish their chores before their guests arrived.

Because they were entertained, I peacefully embraced this time to work on projects that had been neglected. I strolled through the house humming, doing my "Mommy" things, while they were all amused with their company. Little did I realize, this precious quiet time was actually the calm before the storm. I heard a few disturbed voices and then….It ALL BLEW UP! These enraged, crazed little people came storming out of the bedrooms like wild fans at a rock concert. Running, hollering, and trying to scream louder than the next. My peace evaporated as this tornado of untamed fury was unleashed about me. Ear-piercing shrieks of, "We had it first!" "Look what he did!" and "She knows she's not allowed to do that!" erupted in my house.

I began sorting through the lists of furious complaints, as each one pointed out the others wrongdoings and violations. All were worried about what the other group was doing, or not doing. In order to put an end to the controversies, I had to out-yell them, "You just worry about you!!!" I hollered, "I'll handle them!"

As I attempted to resume my peaceful activities, I pondered the words that had just come out of my mouth. Suddenly, I envisioned God sitting in Heaven looking down at me and saying, "Hey, that's really good advice, you just worry about you!"

Surely, I thought, God couldn't be speaking to me. This is about a bunch of kids that won't mind their own business and take care of themselves. I stopped. I put my sewing down. I thought. Yes, this has everything to do with me. I am always talking to my husband, and running to God, with other peoples issues. I'm either feeling sorry for this person or angry at that person. I'm either helping them with problems or allowing them to become my problem. I always think I can fix the world.

Truth is, I have enough trouble with my own life. I'm not in any position to fix the economy; I have enough trouble with my own budget. I'm not in any position to counsel the neighborhood about parenting, even though I sometimes think I have all the answers. I'm not in a position to fix my friends marital problems, even though I think I have attained adequate counseling abilities from afternoon television. I'm not even in a position to fix all that is wrong with my husband, even though if he did what I told him, he'd be perfect.

We have already talked about getting in God's way. This chapter is more about running to God when we don't like what other people are saying and doing. We think we have all the answers. We know what is best for everyone else. We try to run our world, and everyone else in it, according to *our* personal belief system. We find it very easy to measure others according to *our* standards. If people don't do things *our* way, then it's the wrong way! Sometimes, we act like we know everything. Just like my children, we can be equally tempted to point out the wrongdoings and violations of others. When I callously size up a person, they don't stand a chance if they aren't enough like me, or if they don't think enough like me. I never want my children to judge others like that. I don't believe God wants His children to make others feel so inadequate either.

If we keep a list of other peoples offenses, especially those of our spouses, then that list could easily grow daily, maybe even hourly. God knows that it takes practice for us to become good at something, including playing well with others.

God, in his infinite wisdom, decided from the very beginning to allow everyone to choose for themselves. Not only beliefs, but their attitudes and behaviors as well. If God gives all of humanity the right to experience, to learn, and to make their own personal decisions, then who am I to think that I know better? Am I better than God? God did not program us to do everything His way, He wanted us to willingly choose to come to Him and do things His way.

We have a choice to walk in condemnation, to play

God, to pretend that we have the power to judge others, and to point out their inadequacies. We have a choice to exercise judgment on everyone that doesn't think like us. We have a choice to banish those from our lives that don't agree with us.

On the other hand, we also have a choice to walk in love. To accept others for their God-given differences and allow those very differences to compliment us. We have a choice to put others down or encourage them to reach for their dreams. We have a choice to be derogatory toward others or inspire them to reach their potential. Jesus was the perfect example. He always walked in love and the only ones He spoke harshly with were the religious examples of that day. To everyone else, he was their cheerleader. He encouraged, inspired, promoted all to look beyond the obvious, to unlock their potential, to grab on to His hand and go farther in this world than they ever thought possible. When they stepped out in faith, He met them, they joined together, and then....miracles happened! Lives were changed. Those that were lost and hopeless could now live enthusiastically!

How we perceive others is important, but it is also important how we deal with their perception of us. Christians are not immune to offense. So what do we do when others mistreat us, lie to us, misjudge us, use us? I do what my children do, and say, "I'm telling!!!" I go directly to God and tell Him exactly what happened.

A while ago, I was mad at my husband. He didn't like something I said, or did, and he was letting me know about it. He was telling me just what he thought and

I grew more and more angry with his words, his tone, his audacity, and everything else about him. As the situation intensified, I became more enraged at everything he had done wrong in the last twenty years. It had gotten to a point where I had had enough, so I stomped out of the bedroom, slammed the door, and silently screamed, "I'M TELLING JESUS!!"

Typical childish response right? But God does expect us to bring our troubles to Him. The Bible tells us that it's okay to be angry, but don't sin. So I can get angry, then I have to give it to God. Remember, He wants us to cast all of our cares upon Him, even when the problem is our spouse. He really wants to make things right for His children. And He promises to rescue us from our troubles, if we love Him. And to love Him is to obey Him. Psalm 91:14 says, "Because he loves me," says the Lord, "I will rescue him;" In fact, all of Psalm 91 reveals God's protection for those who trust in Him and do things *His* way. If we seek Him, love Him, and obey Him, then all of our needs will be met. We can be *confident* that God will show up on our behalf, if we do things His way.

We have a choice to handle injustice ourselves *or* to let God handle it. If we want the job of dealing with unfair people, then God will let us have the position. But then we have to realize that we have taken the position from Him. He won't show up, because we just told Him we don't need Him. God doesn't compromise; He won't step in and do things our way, only His way. Remember your parents telling you, "it's my way or the highway!" If we want God to come alongside of us, to watch our backs and take care of others for us, then all the scriptures give us the same message, **we have to do it His way!**

I have a friend that is raising a toddler. When the child gets into something the mother doesn't want her to touch she says, "That's not your business!" I laugh at how often she repeats it. It seems, at times, that all she does is chase behind the little girl calling out, "That's not your business!!!" When I am tempted to be judgmental, I need to say to myself, "That's not your business!" If I am allowing God to direct my steps, and my thoughts, then I'm going to hear those words quite often. When a situation doesn't concern me, "That's not your business!!" When God doesn't want me to be involved in a situation, then the Holy Spirit is going to be telling me, "That's not your business!!"

My children frequently say, that God is a God of second chances, third chances, fourth chances, one millionth chances. We keep sincerely saying we're sorry and He keeps sincerely forgiving us. To be like Jesus, is to be a person that offers second chances, third chances, fourth chances…one millionth chances. If people are genuinely sorry, then we are to be as merciful as God, for the amount of mercy He gives us is based on the amount of mercy we are willing to dish out. It really is simple. All we have to do is be willing to progress and willing to forgive. God enthusiastically forgives all of His children and encourages us to press on. We must enthusiastically forgive others and encourage them to press on.

How then are Christians suppose to defend themselves? We are supposed to do exactly what we tell our children to do. Don't start anything and don't cause any trouble! If someone has said something that is untrue about you, then you may kindly go to them and try to settle the situation. If it doesn't work, then give it to God. Remember, God did give us a brain to use. To exercise common sense.

I remember when one of our boys was in school. Two other boys were hitting and kicking him. He fought back in self-defense, and yet he was the one that was disciplined. Upon talking to the teacher, we found out that she thought defending himself was wrong. That's ridiculous! It is **not** a sin to defend yourself or your reputation. It **is** a sin to retaliate. Retaliation is getting even with someone. We would never tell one of our children to stand there and take a beating from a couple of bullies. We do expect our children to never start a fight, and they should do everything in their power to avoid one, but never would we want him, or her, to not defend themselves.

Never does God expect anyone to sit by and be a victim of physical abuse. Turn the other cheek means to ignore an insult, it does not mean we have to kindly smile as someone beats us, or someone we love, to a bloody pulp. I remember teaching my children that little quote, "sticks and stones may break my bones, but names will never hurt me." When Jesus gave us the scripture about turning the other cheek, he was teaching us the same thing. Adults can be as verbally hurtful as some children. He wants us to walk away and not be anxious to retaliate. If someone is going to hurt us, or someone we love, then we need to be responsible and do whatever we can to avoid that situation. If people are in danger because of another persons destructive behavior, then that behavior needs to be dealt with. Remember, God wants the best for us in the same way we want the best for our children. God requires us to forgive and be tolerant of the weaknesses of others, but He does not require us to be tolerant of their abuse.

Each morning I can wake up *confident* that God is going to forgive me when I ask, give me strength when I need it, and handle everything that I can't. He gives me the blessing of taking care of only what I can, and He steps in and does the rest. We have to release others from the responsibility of being perfect and we have to release ourselves from the responsibility of being perfect. We have to forgive others when they mess up and forgive ourselves when we mess up. We have to realize what we *are* responsible for and what we are not responsible for. We *are not* responsible for anyone else's salvation. We are not responsible for anyone else's behavior. We are not even responsible for anyone else's happiness. For these responsibilities, God looks down and says, "You just worry about you."

We are responsible for realizing that other people are just as important to God as we are. We are responsible for encouraging others as Jesus encourages us. We are responsible for realizing that God thinks we are special and is totally committed to working with us and loving us. We are responsible for treating others with the same respect for their choices that Jesus gives us. We are responsible for showing others the compassion and miraculous love of Jesus. We are responsible for walking alongside of God with an enthusiastic smile and a love for what He loves. We are responsible for giving others the same number of chances that God gives us. Millions and millions.

I only have to focus on doing what He tells me to do. Act like Jesus wants me to act. As long as I am going to God and releasing all of my heartaches to Him, as long as I'm focusing on handling my life in a godly way, then God will come to my defense and say, "Don't you worry, I'll handle them!"

I believe God is telling His people that sometimes we are getting involved in things we don't need to be. We are judging what we don't have jurisdiction over. Most of us can't even trust Him enough to handle our **own** lives. We have enough problems working out our own relationship with God. We have enough trouble understanding our own destiny in this world. We have enough issues with ourselves.

God wants us to enjoy others in our lives and encourage them to live a life led by Jesus, but when we don't do that, when we sit in the seat of judgment, God says to us, "You have enough to deal with. You just worry about you!!"

You're Grounded!
Chapter Twelve

"This hurts me more than it hurts you!" "I'm only doing this for your own good!" "I only discipline you because I love you!" "If I didn't care, then I wouldn't bother correcting you!" "One day you'll thank me!" When I was eight, I promised myself that I would never, *ever*, **ever**....under any circumstances....say any of those things to my children! And by the age of twenty-eight, I had said every one of them! Since childhood, however, I've learned that it's not any more fun being on the other end of discipline. Like most parents, we let them get by with only so much and then we deal with the problem. Parents really do discipline children because they love them.

Discipline is loving correction. Depending on the child, we lecture, give timeouts, we ground, and even spank. It's our responsibility to correct behavior that can hurt themselves or hurt someone else. We also have to address direct acts of defiance, since children need to learn to respect authority. Because we want what is best for our children, we lead them down the road by the firm, loving hand of correction. When we direct them, we are preparing them for a healthy physical, mental, emotional, and spiritual walk through life.

When they are newborns we constantly hold them and bond with them. We talk and sing to them because we want our children to know our voice. We take time to play with them and nurture them because we want to establish a relationship of trust and reliance. They soon learn that we are their Mommy and Daddy and understand that we are a constant in their life, regardless of circumstances.

As they grow, they learn how to get along with others, how to respect others and share, and how to be a loving member of the family. When we find approved environments, we put them in situations to practice acceptable behavior. Now they are practicing what we have taught them, exploring new possibilities, and discovering who they are and what they can do. As they study others, follow examples, and make decisions, our children discover trial and error, and success and failure. And through direction and redirection, we are constantly beside them to gently remind them of our expectations. We encourage their strengths and help them deal with their weaknesses. Persistently, parents monitor each childs growth and behavior, carefully watching for any conduct that may potentially threaten the adults that they will one day be. It is our responsibility to teach them healthy responses to adversity and to respect others, so they will grow up being an asset to society and not a burden

When a parent is truly concerned about the future of their child, then correction is inevitable. When we take our children aside for correction, what we are really saying is that they need to stop and reflect. They need some time to think about what is, and is not, acceptable. They need some time to evaluate what is going on in their lives and assess the choices that they have made. They need time to examine what they did right, what they did wrong, and figure out how they could handle things differently. They need time with their parents, without distractions, to review what they have been taught. Many times they get away from the values and closeness of their family and begin adopting the undesirable behaviors and mindsets of others. They need some time to be reminded of what is desirable. If they find themselves in situations that overwhelm them, then those circumstances must be minimized, or removed, in order for them to see clearly. For no one in the world can love them as much as their parents, and they need to stay close and connected to them in order to keep their perspectives clear and healthy. They just need time to talk and work out their issues.

This time doesn't have to be negative. It's a time to encourage them in their uniqueness. A time to strengthen them as they pursue their own personal goals. A time to let them know how much they are loved and valued for who they are. A time to reinforce their understanding that their life is a process of right and wrong choices and that we know they will make mistakes. To let them know that we love them, we just don't love the behavior. Saying, "Hey, you're grounded!!" can actually turn into some very precious time spent together, growing closer. It sounds funny, but our children have actually enjoyed some of our time together during their punishment.

Of course, there are times when they aren't so compliant. Sure, we tell them that we love them too much to allow them to continue doing what they are doing. We just want better for them. Still, they don't seem to ever get excited about punishment. They don't want anyone to correct them and they certainly don't want anyone telling them what to do. Most children think they are always right and they want to do things their way.

We all know what happens to children that receive little or no correction. They are spoiled and being around them can be a challenge. Children that do not have parents nudging them to live at a higher, less selfish, more respectful level, struggle with relationships. Without a healthy respect for authority, there is conflict with their parents as well.

Some parents, however, confuse discipline with abuse. The results of this are children who have social anxieties and anger problems. They wrestle with relationships and seem to either continue on an abusive path or allow themselves to be abused. Because they didn't live within healthy boundaries as children, they have difficulty drawing boundaries as adults.

If we think about it, just as our children's behavior does not always please us, our behavior does not always please God. We can be headed in a direction that God does not want us to go and sometimes He has to step in and stop us from making some big mistakes. It can take some undesirable circumstances to end a relationship that God does not want us in. Sometimes our health changes drastically, to teach us to take better care of ourselves. Sometimes we have to hit bottom, so all we can do is go up. God will let us get by with only so much and then we have to deal with our problems. He wants to correct the behaviors that can hurt us or others, but most of the time, we're not very compliant. We don't want anyone correcting us and we don't want anyone telling us what to do. We have a tendency to think that we are always right and to want to do things our own way!

      God would rather be blessing us, than disciplining us, but He has to address our rebellion and teach us respect for authority. God knows that we need to develop a healthy reverence for Him. Because He loves us, He wants what is best for us. He leads us down the road by the firm, loving hand of correction, in order to prepare us for a healthy physical, mental, emotional, and spiritual walk through life.

      When we first come to the knowledge of God and accept Jesus as our Savior, then He grabs us up, like we do our newborn baby, and keeps us very close to Him. He wants to spend time with us, to bond with us. He wants us to learn His voice, and to establish trust and reliance. He wants us to know that He is a constant in our life, regardless of circumstances.

      As we grow, He starts teaching us acceptable behavior. He teaches us how to get along with others, how to respect others, and how to be part of a loving family. Just like our children, we aren't born knowing everything. Actually, we aren't born knowing much of anything! It's important to God that we know how He wants things done. He wants us to rise to a higher level of living. He wants us to walk on higher ground, to practice walking on the ground that Jesus walked on. He wants us to practice what He is teaching us, to explore all that we can do with Him, and discover how far we can go with Him leading the way.

As we study, follow the examples of Jesus, and make decisions, we discover trial and error, and success and failure. And through direction and redirection, He is constantly beside us to gently remind us of His expectations. To stay close beside Him and to love others....including those that are not easy to love. To be nice to those that are not easy to be nice to. Jesus puts us in specific environments to develop these skills and to learn how to respond to adversity, so we will be an asset to His church, not a burden. He uses the situations in our lives to refine us, to smooth the rough edges of our personalities, and to create more patience and love. He encourages our strengths and helps us deal with our weaknesses. Persistently, God monitors our growth and behavior and carefully watches for any conduct that may potentially harm the great children of God that we were created to be!

Unfortunately, not everyone accepts God's gentle correction. That's why there are so many miserable believers. They may have been in a church pew for thirty years, but are still being grounded for the same thing. They don't move on, they rebel and never realize the abundant life that God created them for. That's why Hosea 4:6 says, "my people are destroyed from their lack of knowledge." They can't enjoy God's best because they are still fighting over parking spots and church decorations. He just wants us to treat people like Jesus treated them. It's that simple, but many can not pass Love 101!!!

Remember when your grade school teacher would say, we're going to do this over and over, until you get it right? God is saying the same thing. We are going to do this over and over, until you get it right! God still loves us, but He can't take us to higher ground until we understand the level we are presently at. I guess I would be pretty miserable, too, if I were grounded for thirty years! But when we refuse to do things God's way, we are not going to get God's blessing, we are going to get God's discipline. We may get to heaven, but we will not enjoy the journey!

We know that our children are going to mess up and God knows that His children are going to mess up, too. When God says, "Hey, you're grounded!" it doesn't have to be negative. We can understand that He is a concerned Father looking out for the welfare of His child. When we have a "timeout" situation, God is getting us by ourselves so we can stop and reflect. He's giving us some time to think about what's going on in our lives. To assess the choices that we have made. What did we do right? What did we do wrong? What could we have done differently? We need time with our Heavenly Father, without distractions, to review what we have been taught. Many times we get away from the values and closeness of our spiritual family and begin adopting undesirable behaviors and mindsets of others. We begin justifying our actions, even when we know they don't line up with God's word. Sometimes our circumstances are so overwhelming that God has to remove us from the situation in order for us to see more clearly. For no one in the world can love us as much as our Father, and He knows we need to stay close to Him and stay connected with Him in order to keep our perspective clear and godly. He knows we are going to simply need some time to talk and work out our issues.

    We have to keep in mind that not all separation in life is grounding. Sometimes it is merely redirection. God wants us to let go of old things so that we can grab on to something new. At first, it may feel like punishment, but when it's over, we can see the gifts that He has given. When we don't see a destination, when we don't see where God is trying to take us, then it's difficult to enjoy change. All we see is what God wants us to give up, to let go of. Sometimes all God wants us to let go of is the way we think. We need to look over that feeling of loss and see what we have to gain. We need to stop crying about what was taken away and look into His other hand for what He's replacing it with. *There is always a prize in the other hand.* Whatever God wants to take out of our lives, He's going to replace with something much, much better. That's why sometimes in our life, our prayers seem to go unanswered. Maybe we have wanted something so desperately, and we have asked and asked God for it. But no matter how much we pray, it doesn't seem as if God is listening. But He is listening! He may be asking you to give up something first. Maybe it's a bad habit, or an addiction. Perhaps God wants us to trade in our negative attitude or develop patience with someone who knows how to get the best of us. He always wants to give us what we want, but we have to be willing to do things His way.

After a long winter last year, we wanted to surprise our kids with a weekend get-a-way. Now, we couldn't tell them what we were doing because they would have driven us crazy until it was time to go. So, we kept the plans hidden. They approached the upcoming weekend in typical fashion. Planning where they were going, who would come over to play, and so on. All of their requests, however, were denied. They kept asking for us to approve the next plan and we kept saying NO! They continued to walk away with puzzled looks and boo-boo lips. They thought they had done something wrong. They couldn't figure out why they were being punished, but once we told them to go pack a bag because we were leaving, they weren't the least bit sorry. We stayed at a motel with a great pool, went to different attractions, and had a wonderful time. On the way home one of the boys said it was the greatest weekend that he ever had. Another said, "Thanks for saying no to our other plans because this was better than I could have ever imagined!"

That's what happens when we let go and trust God. We have to trust that His plans are bigger and better than ours. But if we are so stubborn that we want it our way, then we can miss out on the greatest life we could have, better than we could ever imagine.

I remember when my husband and I first married. I thought it was extreme torture, and unfair punishment, that a newly married couple should be so poor. We didn't have money to do much of anything. We were forced to stay home and just dream of what our lives could be. We quizzed each other about a possible rich aunt that maybe one of us had forgotten about. We anxiously awaited Superbowl Sunday because the Prize Patrol from Publishers Clearinghouse might show up at our door. I was so caught up in what we didn't have that I didn't realize what was happening. My husband and I were spending a lot of time together. We talked and learned about each other. We cuddled on the couch and dreamed together. We learned how the other thought, what they liked and disliked. And **Oh My Goodness**!.... during this time of poverty, and torture, and denial, and fighting, and lots and lots of macaroni and cheese, we became best friends. We learned to depend on each other. I learned how wonderful he is. We learned that there was no one on this earth that could ever share what we did. We became so strong that when attacks against our marriage came, we survived them. We became so solid, that whenever problems came our way, they weren't able to penetrate our relationship. I had prayed for a strong, healthy, loving marriage with the man of my dreams and through those circumstances, I got just that!!! Our situation wasn't a punishment at all. It was an answer to my prayers. I am so glad that God left us alone. I am so glad that God didn't send a rich distant relative to rescue us. He knew that separating us from others and blessing us with plenty of time for each other would take us to a better place than I could have imagined.

We have to be careful to not let our plans dominate us so much that we miss the bigger and better plans of God. We can sit and wallow in self-pity at our circumstances and wonder why God has abandoned us. We can think that what the Bible teaches doesn't really work. We can cry and wail for deliverance. We can pray to be rescued. We can wait and do nothing but sink further into despair. We can question, "God, why aren't you doing anything?" but what we are really saying is, "God, why aren't you doing what I told you to do?" We need to realize that sometimes, God's "nothing" is His "everything!"

We need to keep in mind that our brothers and sisters go through the same things we do. Remember, some of them have been grounded a long time! We need to be compassionate toward them and understand that they are children, too. They were born to God, just as we all were, knowing very little. And we all have to learn. Some just take longer than others and some learn more willingly than others. All of God's children are different and

He deals with each one of us according to our personalities and our purpose.

Do things in your life seem to continually go wrong? Does nothing seem to be going right? Is it one problem after another? Perhaps things are more serious; life, as you know it, just came to a sudden halt. Did your world come crashing in? Did your health change, situation change, finances change? Did a relationship seem to disappear, without reason? Do you feel abandoned?

Whether trials and troubles have come your way, either because your grounded or just being redirected, try to make such times positive. Remember, it is during this time that God encourages our uniqueness. He takes this time to strengthen us as we pursue personal goals. It's time that He lets us know how much we are loved and valued for who we are. A time to reinforce our understanding that our life is a process of right and wrong choices and He knows we will make mistakes. He lets us know that He understands that our behavior is not always going to please Him, but He still loves us anyway. Although He does not excuse our rebellion, He knows we are just children and we get confused. He knows we need to learn to fear Him (meaning to respect Him) because He can read our hearts. The Lord is letting us know, like a concerned Father, that He wants better for us and He loves us too much to allow us to continue acting the way we have been. He loves us too much to allow us to not walk hand in hand with Him. He doesn't want us to wrestle with relationships or to walk in the path of abusive people. He wants us to draw healthy boundaries with everyone. This time can actually become very precious time spent together, growing closer. If you are really trying to get close to God, don't worry, He's not mad at you…..He's not rejecting you…..He loves you…..He just doesn't love the behavior!

Look At Me!
Chapter Thirteen

Today, I decided to replace our normal monotonous pace through a long, dark, winters day, with a splash of life at a nearby indoor pool and hot tub! Little did I know that we were about to encounter more life than I expected. Upon our arrival at the resort, we met up with some third and fourth graders from a local school. Apparently, the school's administration had the *same* cure for dreary seasonal boredom.

As I sent my sons to the boys locker room, my daughter and I began fighting through the crowd of excited girls. They flung clothes and goggles in every direction, with the anticipation of breaking loose into a frenzy of splashing and cannonballs that was sure to release those winter blues. We hugged and kissed all the girls that we had not seen in some time and introduced ourselves to a few new anxious faces.

Because I had a headache that morning, I had decided that I wasn't going to join my children in the water that day. Once I realized the company we were in, I was thankful for that decision! Yes, even headaches can come from the Lord. My plan was to quietly relax by the poolside and plant one eye in a good book, while the other eye followed my kids around the pool.

Once the tranquil waters had been ravaged by over-anxious little people, the greetings and pleasantries took a sharp turn. Dozens of voices battled to out-yell each other. "Hey, Look at ME!" "No, Look at ME, look what I can do!" and "No Mamma, look at ME!!!" As I dodged splashes, my head whipped back and forth like a spectator at a tennis tournament. I quickly came to the conclusion that my quality time with my book, just bounced out of play. I furiously tried to keep up with the belly flops, the attempted summersaults, and doggie paddles that barely kept those little bodies afloat. I chuckled at how proud they were of their attempts and how they saw each acrobatic stunt as a perfected professional feat.

As a child of God, I was able to connect with this personal sense of accomplishment. We can also go around engaging in self-built pride when we do a "little" something for God. We cry, "Look at me, God, I'm teaching Sunday School," or "Look at me, I cooked the best dish at last Sunday's potluck!" What about self-praise like, "Look at me, God, my kids are more holy because we home school!" "Look at me, everyone, I highlight a lot of stuff in my Bible!" God's head must flash from side to side trying to keep up with our self-praises and pats on the back. Just like those children, it doesn't matter how pathetic the attempt, we can still think it's a great feat of personal strength or an accomplished skill that we've mastered in just a few tries.

I wonder, What does God actually think of all this? All of our ritualistic attempts to be what some would call a "good Christian." One of the reasons we go through what we do, is so we will be able to encourage someone else through our experience. Many times God has put it on my heart to spend some time with someone, to give them a shoulder to cry on, but I didn't want to take the time, so I justified my lack of involvement with a little check to help them out during their hard times. I used to think I was so dependable because I was one of the few that would show up for choir and I thought, because of my efforts, I could single handedly carry the sopranos into a heavenly version of "How Great Thou Art." I used to think I was so resourceful because I saved a few pennies a day to send to a starving child in a Third World country, while I spent five times as much on junk food that wouldn't even sustain my own life. I thought I was so trustworthy because I taught a youth class, only to trod on their little hearts with the same monotonous material they had heard for years, instead of taking time to prepare a thoughtful, and challenging, lesson. And let's not forget my mighty, unshakable courage that allowed me to stand up for Jesus….only when it was convenient, not too embarrassing, or politically incorrect.

My thoughts were interrupted by a little girl trying to show me how red her stomach was because of all the belly flops she had done. My little boy pointed to the marks on his belly that he had made and cried, "Aren't they great?" With a smile and a nod of my head, I agreed with him, but I really thought,

*"No, they aren't great, **You Are**! Don't you see I love you, period. Not because of the way you think, not because of what you can do, and not because of the marks you make in this life! I want you to be a warm, loving person that wants to be kind and helpful, just because your heart is that big. I want you to obey me, just because you love me. I want you to be a blessing to others because you have so much that you want to give, not because you're trying to impress anyone or because you want to be noticed. **I just love you because you are mine and I just want you to love me!**"*

When I see my husband walking around the house, aimlessly, or sitting on the couch vegetating, I ask him if there is anything I can do for him. I don't ask him because I want him to think I'm the most wonderful wife in the world, I ask him because I love him and I want to do things for him. I just love to see him happy. Sometimes he will ask me for something, but most of the time, when I ask him if he wants anything he says with a smile, "Just love me!" He's not looking for anything but my affection. It's not how much I can do for him, it's how much I love him that counts.

The Bible tells us that we must be free from all unrighteousness to spend eternity with God. We must be made righteous to see heaven. It does **not** say that we must be **self-righteous** to see heaven. It does **not** say that if we do enough for God, we will be righteous. It does **not** say that we can work for, or buy, our righteousness in order to spend eternity with Him. There is **no** way that we can reach righteousness on our own. God has provided **one** way, and **one** way only, for us to attain this necessary righteousness. When Jesus died on the cross His blood represented our sins, **all** of them. Even the really, really bad ones! As His blood spilled from His body, all our sin went with it. And although He did it for everyone, we don't just automatically get it. We have to ask for it. First, we have to realize the sin that spilled out of Him **belonged to us** because we know, from scripture, that Jesus was **sinless**. We have to tell Jesus that we understand, that because He did this, we don't have to live the life we are living. He can save us from wasting our lives on a life of sin, a life without Him. We can have a new life. A different life. We have to tell Him that we believe He is the only way we can have righteousness and that we can't ever see heaven without Him. We have to be sincere. We have to understand that a new life comes with a new mind, a new heart, and a new way of living. And because we believe in Him we will be able to allow Him to lead us as our life changes. Jesus will lovingly change us into the person God created us to be. Matthew 16:25 and 26 says, "For whoever wants to save his life will lose it, but whoever loses his life for me will find it. What good will it be for a man if he gains the whole world, yet forfeits his soul? Or what can a man give in exchange for his soul?"

After we invite Him to change our lives, God sees us differently. When He looks at us He doesn't see our sin, any of it! He only sees the righteousness of Jesus. Jesus covered us completely, inside and out, with Himself, and that is the only way we are righteous.   You see, it wasn't because of anything that we did. It was all because of what Jesus did!

Many people that have already accepted Jesus as their Savior, seem to mix up the righteousness of God, the love of God, and the favor of God. We know that righteousness is reached through Jesus and we can't do anything on our own to attain it. The love of God naturally comes from Him, as our Father. My children can't make me love them, I just do because they are mine.

The favor of God is the blessing of God. Favor can be defined as privileged, preferred, approved of, partial to. Psalm 5:12 says, "For surely, O Lord, you bless the righteous; you surround them with your favor as with a shield." Also in the Old Testament we find that God was so pleased with Abraham's obedience He referred to Himself as Abraham's shield. We can gain or loose the favor of God by our actions, by what we do or don't do. We know that if we want God's protection, then we have to be doing things His way. Obviously, if we are not doing as God would like us to, then He isn't going to rain favor down upon us. But if we are obedient, then we know the favor of God will rain down on us. Isaiah 1:19 says, "If you are willing and obedient, you will eat the best from the land;" We have to be both willing **and** obedient to have God's best. *Favor is conditional. Our Salvation is not.* My children may be kind and considerate children, but if they aren't acting kindly and considerately, then we're going to have a little talk about their behavior. We may be righteous in the eyes of God, but if we don't act righteous, like God wants us to, then He's going to talk to us about our behavior. It doesn't mean that we are not one of His children, it just makes us one of His misbehaving children.

When I look into the face of my children, I honestly love them because they are mine. When I look into the beautiful eyes of my husband, I honestly love him because he is mine. When God looks at His children, those of us that are made righteous through Jesus, He honestly loves us just because we are His. Our value is not in what we do or do not do. Our value is not in what we are capable or not capable of. Our value is not in what we have or do not have. Our value is in Him, because there is nothing that He can not do.

Yes, we are to teach Sunday School, be in the choir, or go to a certain church, **if** God tells us to. We are always to encourage others. But what God is really looking for, is our affection. Beginning a relationship with Him is not about how much we can do for him, it's about how much we love Him. When we get confused and do all kinds of crazy things, thinking we are pleasing God...when we are trying to win God's love, or impress Him...when we are trying to show God the marks we are making in this life while crying out, "Look at me, aren't they great?" I think He says,

"No, they aren't great, You Are because I made you that way! Don't you see I love you, period. Not because of the way you think, not because of what you can do, and not because of the marks you make in this life! I want you to be a warm, loving person that wants to be kind and helpful, just because your heart is that big. I want you to obey Me, just because you love Me. I want you to be a blessing to others because you have so much that you want to give, not because you're trying to impress anyone or because you want to be noticed. I know you want to please Me, but I just love you because you are Mine and I just want you to love Me!"

You Did All This For Me?
Chapter Fourteen

For our anniversary this year, my husband and I went away for a well-deserved restful weekend. Just the two of us. Alone. Really Alone! As we kissed the kids good-bye and threw our bags into the truck, the children waved and yelled, "Have a good time." "Don't worry about anything." And "We have everything under control."

We had a wonderful weekend. We ate at restaurants that didn't have a cute kid's menu. We peacefully sipped coffee on our balcony overlooking a gorgeous pink sunset. We watched some television that didn't feature cartoons. And we lazily shriveled our fingers and feet in a steaming hot Jacuzzi.

One of the best things about the weekend though, was when we returned home. Our wonderful, *beautiful*… **thoughtful**…***EXCEPTIONAL*** children had a fresh pot of coffee waiting for us, a meticulously clean house, and a painstakingly clean garage! I couldn't believe my eyes! The garage hadn't been cleaned in, well, too long for me to mention.

But it was swept, organized, and you could find everything! They even built me a desk with task lighting and a little radio to listen to while I worked on projects. It was unbelievable to see how perfect it was. I guess it's even more unbelievable that three kids would voluntarily do such a thing. Tears filled my eyes as I cried, "You did all this for me?"

"We just wanted to make you happy," they glowed. They were so excited as they told us how much work they had put into it. They worked tirelessly both days and well into both nights.

Recently, I had a birthday and since we're on a pretty tight budget, I didn't really expect too much. We now home school all of our children and the copier that we had rummaged from a church's "get rid of pile" had finally died. My oldest son was the only one with a computer and a printer that worked, so I was forever trying to work out a schedule with him to do my work on his computer. I also wanted to work on this book, so finding time to allow the kids to be on the computer, me to do the school work and make copies on the printer, and to write was becoming rather perplexing. My husband could see that the school work and tests that needed to be made were piling up and that this writing project was never going to be finished.

One Sunday afternoon, after church, my husband told me he was going into town to get some fishing supplies that he needed. I was at the other end of the house when he returned. He kept the kids quiet and when I walked into the living room there sat a huge box sporting….a brand new computer! I stood in awe! No more standing in line waiting for my turn. No more wanting to take a sledge hammer to the copier. No more having things to write about and not being able to work on it. Once again, I couldn't believe my eyes. I looked at him and said, "I can't believe you did all this for me!"

When I think back on both of these occasions, and many others, I realize that when people love you and truly want to show you, they give you exactly what you need. Both gifts were perfect. Saving mom any time is a perfect gift and the kids knew that a clean house and a clean garage would be a perfect gift for me. My husband knew that giving me the tools to get my work done would be another perfect gift for me.

This reminds me of how God treats us. The Bible says all perfect gifts come from God. When I think of all the perfect gifts God has given me I am amazed. He knew me before He even created me. He knows me better that I even know me. He knew what I would like and what I would be like, at every age. He knew how I would develop from one stage of life to the next. He knew exactly what I would be interested in and what I would shy away from. He knew where to put me and when to put me there. He knew what experiences in my life would persuade me to think and believe the way I do. He knew what expectations and needs I would have and gave me a husband that is a perfect compliment. He knew that I loved the change of seasons so He planted me in Michigan where I get to experience them all. He knew how eccentric I would be and sent me very interesting, weird friends. He knew that I would like to work in the garden, even before I knew it, and planted me in a perfect spot to grow roses. He knew I would like the country, better than the city, and gave my family lots of room to run and play. He knew my husband would like to fish and moved us to a land of many lakes. He knew my children would like the snow, so He gave us a ski resort just three miles from our home. He knew that I would love being a mom, and He gave me three children. Three really good ones! He knew that I would want to teach my children, so He provided a way for us to home school. He knew that my husband would one day want to be an electrician, so He planted us in a place very close to his work and school.

Most importantly, He knew that I would sometimes mess up....O.K.....I would mess up a lot. And I would need His forgiveness. With all my responsibilities, the kids activities, home school, church, and everything else, He also knew that it would be difficult to find the time to slaughter an animal for sacrifice, build an altar, and go through the rituals of the Old Testament. He also knew that I would have a hard time with all the laws of that day. I mean, stop signs and speed limits are really pushing it! So He sent a very simple gift, that was absolutely perfect, in every way. He sent Jesus to be the ultimate sacrifice so all I had to do is ask for forgiveness and He would always be faithful to forgive me. And I thought my family went out of their way to please me. God thought enough…of me…to sacrifice His only Son. He really has taken the time to know me and has made **all** the arrangements for my fulfillment, in this life and the next.

I have to admit, that sometimes along the way, I felt that God wasn't even listening to my prayers. But actually, He was working out every little, tiny detail to give me exactly what I needed. He wants to please me, so much, that He doesn't overlook the smallest aspect of a gift. It's the moments in my life when I felt my prayers were ignored, that I can see….He was simply working out the details. Whatever He was working on for me had to be absolutely perfect. The right people had to be in place. The right objects had to be set up and obstacles had to be removed. The timing had to be just right. The weather, the day, the hour….everything meticulously orchestrated so that when He was done with the gift, I could look up to heaven and tell everyone what **He did** for me.

It's kind of funny now, but there were times when I looked at my life and wondered…*why, God, why?* We don't always understand what is best for us.   Sometimes, that blessing comes disguised. If I would quit throwing a fit long enough, then I could see that many of the thorns in my side were attached to a perfect rose. We should be awestruck and thankful at how detailed God is, not irritated with Him for it.

In Matthew 7:11 we find, " If you, then, though you are evil, know how to give good gifts to your children, how much more will your Father in heaven give good gifts to those who ask him!" When I'm feeling overwhelmingly grateful, like right now, I look up to heaven and can just imagine God's face glowing as He says, "I really want you to be happy! Please, don't worry about anything, I've got everything under control!"   That's when I stand captivated by His love and all I can say is, "I can't believe, God, You did all this for me!"

Is This Your Best?
Chapter Fifteen

We had some pretty bad cases of spring fever that day. Well, it was more like that week. The snow had melted and everything was pretty slushy, but it didn't seem to matter to them. To those three children.... the muddier, the sloppier, the better! Their eyes were wide with anticipation as they focused on the back door, instead of their books. They sat on the edge of their school chairs ready to jump out of those seats the minute I gave the O.K. Once I said they could go, they about knocked me over trying to bust through the door. The sounds of basketballs bouncing, of laughter as they rode against the wind on their bikes, and of an old hammer trying to repair the winter damage to their fort, was welcome.

While my restless children said goodbye to winter, I grabbed a fresh cup of coffee and a pile of papers that needed to be graded. I sat down and frowned at the first paper, it was so messy. I made a face at the next... and the next. I skipped a few and found sloppy work toward the bottom of the pile, as well. This wasn't acceptable. Some didn't even bother erasing mistakes, they just wrote the new answer over the old one! As I rummaged through the pile, it was one example after another of messy, incomplete work. The more I heard that hammering, the more irritated I became. This isn't their best, it's not even close! It would be fine if they just made some mistakes or didn't understand the material, but that was obviously not the case. They…Didn't…Even… TRY!

I stewed for a while as I watched them out the window. I was too mad to go get them. I knew they would come in eventually….when they got hungry! Eventually they came in. I marched them over to the couch and lined them up!

"Uh-oh!" they whimpered. They didn't even look at me. They knew what this one was all about before it even started. I began by waving their papers in the air, and with one hand on my hip, I executed the classic, "Is this your best?" speech with unsurpassed attitude. I watched their little beady eyes dart around the room, but oh no, they weren't going to get by with that.

"You look at me when I'm talking to you. *"I don't expect you to get everything right. But I expect you to try. I don't expect you to always feel like doing what you are told, but I do expect you to work on that little attitude and do it regardless of how you feel. I don't expect you to agree with everything I say, but I still expect you to do it because I'm the Momma, and I have a plan, and I know what I am doing. And I am doing more than just educating you. I take my time to personally instruct you so you learn to live an extraordinary life, not just an ordinary one. To do more. To be more. To strive for more. My children will be leaders, not followers. My children will be warriors, not whiners. My children will walk in victory, not in defeat. My children will overcome adversity, not bow down to it. My children will embrace opportunity, not run from it. My children will master their lives, not be mastered by them. My children will wake up each day excited about new challenges, not dreading them. I will never reward lazy work. I will never pat you on the back for a job on which you didn't give your all. I will never feed your selfishness. And I will never encourage you to fall short of your dreams. I love you far too much for that!!*

Everything that I do is to teach you...to prepare you... to equip you...for a life where you can reach your fullest potential. A life so wonderful that all the godly desires of your heart are met. So if this is your best work....If this is your best effort....If you honestly can not do any better....then you are free to go. You can just get up off that couch expecting the rest of your life to be nothing more than a growing list of unfulfilled dreams and prayer requests at church."

They looked at each other, then back to me, saying nothing. Since my husband is a former Marine, I took the concept of recruiting a "Few Good Men" to another level. I looked at those three little faces and with the determination of drill instructor I lowered my voice as deep as I could and slowly questioned, *"IS...THIS...YOUR...BEST?"*

"No," they responded in unison.

"With God, my children can do anything!" "With God,

my children can go anywhere!" "*With God*, my children can conquer anything!" "*ARE YOU MY CHILDREN?*"

"Yes!" they all shouted.

I threw my arms around them and ordered, **"Then get up and act like it!!"**

They scattered to retrieve their books and papers so they could redeem themselves. I thought out loud "Lord, this reminds me of the last time they cleaned their rooms. Remember when I went in to inspect their work and they had shoved dirty clothes into boxes and toys under the bed. Remember when I had to ask them, if this was their best?"

Then God said, **"Let me tell you, what this reminds me of!"**

"Uh-oh," I whimpered.

"Remember, last month when I told you to put a little extra in the offering plate at church? Accompanied by dozens of excuses, you didn't. Then you felt guilty for not doing it so you gave it to another ministry, one that I didn't tell you to, just to satisfy your own conscience. Remember the other day when I told you to call someone that was going through a really bad time, but you didn't know what to say, so you pretended to be too busy to make the call. Remember that person you saw in the market, a while back, the one I told you to invite to church, but you weren't real sure if she would appreciate the invitation, so you decided to do it another time, when it would look better for you. Remember when your husband came home from a long, long, long day at

work and needed a back rub and some attention, and you just didn't feel up to it. At any time...do you recall...a friend calling you, over and over, trying to reach you, and you not bothering to return the call?

Let's reminisce back to your working days. Did you always give your best to your boss, show up on time, focused, to work a full shift? Is your house clean? Laundry done and put away? If you can not run your own household...if you can not keep your own affairs straight...if you can not take care of your own business...then you don't need to be involved in anyone else's business! I don't believe you have been even close to your best. Why do you refuse to take care of what I have already given you, and then turn around and ask for more?

It would be fine if you just made some mistakes, or didn't understand, but it's not about mistakes. You know I don't get mad when you make mistakes. This is all about you not trying. Oh, I see your eyes darting around the room, but oh no, I'm not going to let you get by with that. You look up at me when I'm talking to you.

I don't expect you to get everything right. But I expect you to try. I don't expect you to always feel like doing what I tell you, but I expect you to work on that little attitude and do it regardless of how you feel. I don't expect you to agree with everything I say, but I still expect you to do it because I'm the Father...and I have a plan...and I know what I am doing. And I am doing more than just educating you. I don't want you to live an ordinary life...I want you to live an extraordinary life. To do more. To be more. To strive for more. My children are leaders, not followers. My children are warriors, not whiners. My children walk in victory, not defeat. My children will overcome adversity, not bow down to it. My children will embrace opportunity, not run from it. My children will master their lives, not be mastered by them. My children will wake up each day excited about new challenges, not dreading them. I will never reward your lazy work. I will never pat you on the back for a job on which you didn't give your all. I will never feed your arrogance. I will never encourage you to over commit yourself. I love you far too much for that.

I did not send my only Son into this world to be abused, beaten, walked on, spit on, tortured, and killed...FOR NOTHING!!! Yes, He died because He loves you. Yes, He died so you could have the perfect plan of redemption. But....He died for even more. He died so you can be healed. He died so you don't have to be sick. So you could overcome weakness. So you could live in freedom. So you could get rid of all that baggage you have been carrying around with you. So you could be empowered by the Holy Spirit, capable of doing all things through Him. He died so you could rise above mediocrity. So you could rise above the average and live a life of excellence. So there can be godly fathers, and godly mothers, raising godly children. So you can have the strength to have a clean house, clean kids, a clean husband, and still have the time, the energy, the desire to serve God's people. He died so men could have the ability to be strong, dependable husbands and women could become sensitive, desirable wives. So you can be a model businessperson. So you can be a pillar in your community. So you can be a trustworthy employee and coworker. My Son died so you would never, ever be just another face in the crowd!! He died so you could have your cake and eat it too! He died so you would be recognized EVERYWHERE YOU GO, as a child…OF ALMIGHTY GOD! The child…that I created you to be! And the child…that Jesus died for you to be!

In John 10:10 I told you why Jesus came, "The thief comes only to steal and kill and destroy; I have come that they may have life, and have it to the full."

Everything that I do is to teach you…to prepare you…to equip you…for a life that reaches its fullest potential. So if this is your best work…If this is your best effort…If you honestly can not do any better… than you are free to go. You can just get up off that couch expecting the rest of your life to be nothing more than a growing list of unfulfilled dreams and prayer requests at church.

Now you look into the eyes of my Son, the Son I sacrificed for you, and answer the question, "IS…THIS…YOUR…BEST?"

"No," I shamefully responded.

"With Jesus, my children can do anything! With Jesus, my children can go anywhere! With Jesus, my children can conquer anything!! ARE YOU MY CHILD?"

"Yes," I cried.

"Then Get…Up…And…Act…Like…It!!

You're Gonna Get It!
Chapter Sixteen

"THAT'S IT!!" ***"YOU…JUST WAIT….UNTIL YOUR FATHER GETS HOME!!!"***

Those words! Those dreadful…awful…*terrifying* words! Few words can torture a kid's soul like that fatal classic expression, "Wait till your father gets home!" I remember sitting in my bedroom, awaiting my impending doom, while my brother and sister would taunt me as they sang, "You're gonna get it! You're gonna get it!" I remember my sister sliding a list under the door of all my stuff she wanted after Dad killed me. My brother was a little more sympathetic, at least he was sorry I'd be gone. However, he was comforted by the thought of an extra pork chop at dinner.

The two hours until Dad got home felt like two years. I paced for a while as I tried to accept my fate. For I knew, beyond a shadow of a doubt that this…was…it! The end of the line. It was a shame to have to go at such a young age. After I accepted my destiny, I tried to imagine how it would happen. How would the punishment be executed? Would it be quick and painless? Maybe…slow…and…excruciating! After a few minutes of graphic agony, my thoughts switched to how sorry they would be after they did it! Oh yeah, they would be sorry!!! What if I got the black plague or something? They would never forgive themselves for their cruelty. They would cry in shame for every punishment they ever gave me!!

The hands on the clock hardly seemed to move. I thought about it and decided that, although my life was about to end, two hours was more than enough time to plan a funeral. I made a list of all the people I wanted, and didn't want, at the service. It was going to be by invitation only. And I definitely was **not** inviting my sister! And when it was Dad's turn to kill her I wasn't coming to her little ceremony, either!

Just then, I heard the car pull into the driveway. My eyes widened as I looked out the window to see Dad turn off the ignition and step out of the vehicle. I swallowed hard. As I heard the screen door slam shut, I shuddered, as it signified the premature end of my young life. I envisioned my scowling mother standing in the kitchen in her frilly apron, with a hand on her hip, waving a wooden spoon around as she described my fiendish behavior. **Traitor**!! I couldn't even remember what I did wrong as I heard the mammoth footsteps grow closer. Beads of sweat formed on my little forehead as my last few heartbeats pounded through my head. My fate was being sealed as I watched the doorknob slowly turn. With one last breath of freedom I looked up, staring certain death in the face, to bravely receive my life sentence. My Dad's mouth opened and

the words that passed his lips will forever ring in my ears…………..
With little expression he said, "Just don't do it again." Then he turned…and left….shutting the door behind him.

That's it? With a stupid look of bewilderment on my face, I fell back on the bed. That's it! "Just don't do it again!" What??? No flogging….no explosives….no press? It was almost disappointing. And it was going to be such a *nice* funeral, too! Puzzled, I kept repeating, "Just don't do it again?" "Just don't do it again?"

I tried. I really did. But I just couldn't leave it alone. I marched out of that bedroom, down those stairs, into the den, and yanked on his shirt sleeve. "What do you mean, just don't do it again?" I sputtered. "I don't get it, why aren't you mad at me?"

As he slowly pulled the newspaper away from his face, he frowned down at me and sternly responded, "Do you want me to be?"

"Well, no, but I don't understand why I'm not in trouble," I humbly replied.

He said kindly, "Up until now, I know that you didn't understand. You didn't know any better. But now you do. I'm giving you a choice to change what you are doing."

He never reminded me of the incident. He never rubbed it in my face. In fact, it was never mentioned again.

To this day I don't remember why I got in trouble, but I sure do remember my Dad's response. His reaction caused me to change how I looked at him. I had a new respect for him. I found myself thinking before I did something simply because I wanted to please him. I didn't want to disappoint him. Somehow…I think I even loved him more! He didn't change any. I did. The change came from within me because I knew something I didn't know before. Now, I didn't do things just because I was supposed to, I did them because I wanted to.

We read a similar story in John 8. A bunch of teachers of the law brought a woman caught in the act of adultery to Jesus. They wanted her stoned to death because that was the penalty for such a crime in those days. This is when Jesus coined the phrase, "If any one of you is without sin, let him be the first to throw a stone at her."

I can just see them all standing in front of the Lord, waiting for someone to speak up. For one of them to think they qualified, but not one of them could. They knew they were in front of the Holy One. Although they had plenty of self-righteousness, they knew none among them were without sin. They all left. As amazing as it may be for a bunch of self-righteous religious junkies to walk away from a perfectly good stoning, even more amazing to me is what Jesus said next. He asked the woman if anyone had condemned her and she said, "NO." In verse 11 it says "...Then neither do I condemn you," Jesus declared. "Go now and leave your life of sin."

That's it!! Her moment of truth had come. And the beautiful thing is that it came without condemnation. It was time for her to make a choice.

I can only imagine what went through her mind that day. She must have been scared to death as these men grabbed her and dragged her off for sentencing. It doesn't say how far they had to walk to find Jesus, but I bet that it felt like a lifetime to her. I'm sure they weren't at a loss for words as they journeyed for justice. I can hear them scornfully curse her as they repeat, "You are **really** gonna get it!" She was probably terrified, as each step brought her closer and closer to her end. She knew the law, she had been taught since she was just a girl. Beyond a shadow of a doubt, she knew, this was the end of the line. Her life would soon be over. As the group approached the crowd around Jesus, she wondered how long would it take? Would it be quick….and….painless? Would it be slow….and….agonizing? It was bad enough to have been caught, but to be paraded in front of the King of Kings. I can imagine her taking her last breath of freedom as she looked up into the eyes of the Holy Son of God, into the eyes of the King that would seal her fate. Beads of sweat formed on her forehead, as she guiltily looked up at Him. The moment must have seemed to last a lifetime, as she watched His mouth open and heard the words that would ring in her ears forever. "Go and sin no more!" "Just don't do it again!"

      What did she think, when she looked into those heavenly eyes and didn't find any condemnation?….Only compassion! And although it doesn't say it in the Bible, I can just picture Him gently taking her worried face in His hands and saying, "Go and just don't do it again!" You probably could have knocked her over with a feather! The Lord wanted to **SAVE** her life, not end it! He told her to, " Go!" meaning turn in a new direction. All she had to do was turn and her life was spared. I bet she stopped what she was doing, not just because it was the right thing to do, *but because she wanted to*! Maybe she just *couldn't* bear the thought of disappointing Him again. Somehow, did that change who she was? Did a change rise up within her because she discovered something....something she hadn't known before....God's mercy?

One day, each one of us will stand before Jesus, the Holy Son of God. Time will seem to stand still as we recount our life. All of our thoughts....all of our words....all of our acts!!! We will recall hearing the message that we had to have Jesus in order to be righteous. We will remember that we were told, at some time in our lives, that we needed to make that decision, just like that woman. That decision that began with, "Go and sin no more!" She had to decide, which way she was going to turn. Turn back and not change anything or turn in the opposite direction and change how she thought, how she felt, and how she lived.

Everyone has to decide for themselves which way they are going to turn. Jesus promised that if we chose Him, chose to mimic His life, that all of our sin would be erased. Forgotten. Never will God rub our past in our face. In fact, it will never be mentioned again. But we have to turn in God's direction, not only because it's the right thing to do, but because we want to!! Because we just don't want to disappoint Him anymore. Only then can we be sure that our name is written in the Book of Life. The book that Jesus opens on Judgment Day. The very book that will...or will not...spell out...your name.

On that day, Satan is going to bring up every thought we have ever had, every word that has passed our lips, and every act we have ever committed and he is going to parade them before the King of Kings. Jesus will look at us.....then into that book.....then back at us. If a person's name is written in it, He will smile and gently stretch out His arms saying, "Well done, good and faithful servant." Satan, like those old Pharisees, will have no choice but to walk away in defeat.

BUT….No matter how good a person was, if their name is not in that book, then Jesus will look at Satan and say, "Yeah, I remember…..I remember everything!" Then He will look at them in disappointment and say as the tears flow down His cheeks, "Depart from Me, I never knew you!" That means that because you didn't have anything to do with Me down there, on earth, I can't have anything to do with you up here. And that was the choice **you** made.

Without Jesus….without the cross He died on….their foreheads will bead up with sweat as they take their last deep breath of freedom and Satan drags them away, laughing at their sentencing. Singing, "You are really gonna get it!"

I'm Not Talking To You!
Chapter Seventeen

I love my children with all my heart and I want nothing more than to see them happy. It is one of my deepest desires to please them and to watch them live contented, successful lives. But despite my efforts, occasionally I make them mad. Occasionally...I make them *really, really* mad.

My children sure were mad at me the other night. I told them that their chores had to be done before they could go out. Well, they didn't have them done in time, so they couldn't go where they wanted. When I handed down the sentence, their footsteps sounded like thunder as they stormed away, pouting. They didn't want to hear me! They didn't want to look at me! They didn't even want to think about me!

Believe it or not, I actually made my children mad again. I told them if they wanted to go to the movies, then they had to earn the money to go. I gave them multiple opportunities to earn the money. I even made a little "Help Wanted" sign with job opportunities and how much each task paid. They kept saying "No," they didn't want the work. They procrastinated until the day of the movies and then stood in astonishment as I told two of them that they couldn't go. They were furious with me because I didn't allow them to do what they wanted, even though I warned them of the repercussions in advance. I believe I even saw fire coming out of their little ears as they pounded off to their rooms. Again, they didn't want to speak to me or have anything to do with me.

One day, I heard two of them fighting. The fight ended with some slammed doors and "I'm not talking to you!!" Well, that's enough of that, I decided, and went to put an end to the "I'm not talking to you anymore" syndromes. It's fine to take some time to cool off, to put yourself in timeout so you won't over react. But I have seen too many people yell, "I'm not talking to you!!" and mean it....for life. They turned around AND NEVER LOOKED BACK. I've seen many people hang on to resentment as they disposed of a family member or a good friend that they were mad at. Because they didn't agree with someone, they were unwilling to acknowledge that person again.

People are not disposable. Let's think about this a little bit more. One of the reasons that we have so much divorce is because it's so easy for people to walk away and not look back. That person to whom they once pledged their undying love became disposable. I've seen fathers and mothers walk away from their children and never look back because they have little understanding of commitment or obligation. Things that are disposable have little to no value. Because some individuals have trouble seeing the value in others, they continually abuse people and don't think that there is anything wrong with it. One of the reasons we have so much discrimination is because often people don't see the value in others. They aren't important. They are disposable. And citizens from one country murder innocent people, from a neighboring country because they got mad and said, "I'm not talking to you anymore." In other words, things didn't go my way and now your life has no value to me.

To some, saying "I'm not talking to you," and meaning it, is acceptable. I assure you it is not acceptable to God. The Bible teaches us to be angry, but don't sin. Don't let the sun go down on your anger. God knows that we have emotions. He gave them to us, but He doesn't necessarily want us to always react with emotion. He wants us to make careful decisions not rash, stubborn, decisions. God never approves of treating people like they are something you can throw away. In fact, it's the opposite of forgiveness. Even people that God does want us to avoid, still have value. They are still His creations. All people have value to God and we should have the same view.

When my children get mad at me, or someone else, they will cross their arms, put on a pouty face, and refuse to acknowledge that person. They don't care who that other person is. They are so mad that they don't feel that person deserves to be acknowledged anymore. It's one way they respond to things not going their way. Their behavior lets me know they are mad at me and that whatever I said or did made them unhappy. But I have news for them. I am not responsible for their happiness. And neither is anyone else. The only ones responsible for their happiness is them. Each person is responsible for the condition of their attitude. And refusal to talk to someone, beyond a reasonable time-out, is nothing but manipulation. By banishing me from their conversations, they feel that they may get me to change my mind. By playing on my feelings of abandonment, they hope I will give in and do things their way. And because I love them, they feel they have the power to control me with emotion.

How do I know it's manipulation? Because if I changed my decision and gave them what they wanted they would gasp in delight, throw their arms around me, and once again proclaim their love for me. Their prolonged withdrawal, is my cue to show up with another one of my Mommy talks:

"I know you're mad, but I've laid out the rules because I know what's best for you. Whether you admit it or not, I made the consequences of your decisions known. I'm sorry you didn't get your way, but there are more people in this house besides you and, contrary to popular belief, the world doesn't revolve around you. I'm the Momma and I am not going to bow to your pressure. Your little tantrum is not going to make me change my mind and your withdrawal is not going to make me change my plans for raising you. So......get over it!"

Many people, reading this, are mad at God. And they are doing the same thing to Him. When things don't go our way or we don't get what we prayed for....we can be pretty quick to point a finger at God and withdraw.

We have to understand that just because we become adults does not mean that the "battle of wills" stops. We still go head to head with others, only we aren't as quick to forgive as we use to be. In preschool, somebody could steal your cupcake on Tuesday and by Wednesday morning they were your 'bestest' friend again. As we grow older, I think it becomes harder to forgive people for "cupcake stealing." Go ahead and take the last one in my house and see just how long I can hold a grudge. But that's not part of God's plan. That's when we put our will before God's will.

We have a big battle of wills going on. First, we have the supreme will of God; the implementation of God's perfect plan in our lives. Then we have our own will and our own idea of what we want. Next, we have the will of other people in our lives and what they want for themselves, and from us. Finally, we have the will of Satan. Of course, he has to put his two cents in. That's a whole lot of people trying to get their own way.

God knows we are not always going to like what happens in our lives. And we will never have to look very hard to find sadness and misery. That's why we are responsible for our own attitude. Each day we choose a positive or a negative outlook. No one else chooses for us. It is not the fault of anyone else if we are miserable. It's our choice. Our fault. We are not responsible for what others do to us, but we are responsible for our reaction. Emotion is a God given reaction to our thinking. To our attitude. It was not designed to control us, or to be used to control others.   Still, many people have fallen into the trap of waiting for the arrival of their contentment.   They say, "I'll be happy when this happens, or when that happens."   "I'll be satisfied when I have this or that."   But those are never-ending lists.   If you are miserable its because you *choose* to be miserable. If all you can do is exist, then that is the choice you made. When God gave us an attitude, He gave us a gift that no one could ever steal from us, or manipulate, without our permission. No one, not even Satan, can steal your joy, or your peace, without your consent.

If you are one of those who have handed your thoughts over to the enemy and are sinking deeper and deeper in despair, then stop trying to take others with you.   It's true that misery loves company, but that is certainly not God's wish for anyone. And only **you** can say when enough is enough. It will only stop when **you** recognize your value in Christ. By retreating from family, friends, church.....by trying to manipulate others through your withdrawal....the one that is most hurt is **YOU**.   Get right with others.   Get right with God. And if necessary, please realize that God wants us to get the spiritual and professional help we sometimes need, too.   It is not a sin to need some godly guidance and direction.   But God leaves that choice up to each person.   Remember, however, we will never conquer battles we do not face.   You can't win a war you don't show up for!

God loves His children with all His heart and wants to see them happy. He wants to please them and to watch them live successful lives. But, despite His efforts, occasionally they get mad. Occasionally, they get *really, really,* mad. God's two most important commandments were to love Him and to love others, so He's not going to think too much of us treating others like they are disposable. He knows that we can have many different responses to disappointment, but through His power, He expects us to overcome our setbacks and not let our emotions control us, or anyone else. As a loving Father He has a similar message to His children that have held on to anger for too long:

> *"I know you're mad, but I've laid out the rules because I know what's best for you. Whether or not you admit it, I made the consequences of your decisions known. I'm sorry you didn't get your way, but there are more people in this world besides you. And contrary to popular belief, the world doesn't revolve around you. I'm the Father and I am not going to bow to your pressure. Your little tantrum is not going to make me change my mind and your withdrawal is not going to make me change my plans for the universe. So....get over it!"*

Who's Your Daddy?
Chapter Eighteen

I love to look at the face of a child when you ask them about their Daddy. Their eyes widen and brighten, their chests puff out, and they expose little missing teeth encircled by a juice-stained grin. If you ask more than one child at a time, "Who is your Daddy?" a roar of responses will flow off their tiny tongues. You quickly realize that these small people are not at a loss for words. Each one tries to get a word in edgewise, while letting all the others in the room know that their father is better than the next. The voice levels continue to rise as you hear, "My father's the strongest!" "My Dad's the nicest!" "My Daddy's the smartest!" "My Dad's the biggest and can beat all your Dad's up!" And, "My Dad can do anything!"

When asked about what kind of work their father does, shouts crescendo as you hear "My Daddy's a doctor!" "My father builds houses!" Mine is an electrician!" "My father's a boss!" "My Dad's a policeman!" And once again, "My Dad can do anything!"

The contest peaks with the question, "What does your father do for you?" Little voices scream, "He gives me stuff!" "He makes me feel better when other kids are mean to me!" "My Daddy takes care of me!" "He protects me!" "He takes me places!" "My Dad makes me happy!" And "My father loves me!"

Their enthusiasm is refreshing and the best part is that each one believes that their father is the best in whole wide world; and that's a really big place to a four year old. As we chuckle at their passionate devotion and allegiance to their fathers, we see that because they love, and are loved so much, they are heirs to success and greatness.

There comes a point in this session, however, that you must look over the heads of that inspiring group of dedicated preschoolers, praising the patriarchs of the family, and notice the group that assembled themselves outside the frenzied circle. This group doesn't share the common bond that the others did. This group is larger. Their little eyes aren't full of excitement and there are no enthusiastic grins or adoring words rushing off their tongues. These are the children that are suffering because they come from dysfunctional, broken, or abusive homes. Some have been lied to, used, and abused. Some have been abandoned and left with no father to turn to. They can become introverted, violent, angry. As we look at their distress, we see that they are heirs to death and destruction.

I am so thankful that God allows us to be His children. We can be born again, washed, cleansed, purified, sanctified, and covered with the blood of Jesus. And because of this, we are made righteous and Holy in the eyes of God. That is definitely not something I can do on my own. So, because I am His child, let me tell you about my Father. My Father is the strongest. He is a rock. In Hebrew, He is called El Shaddai, meaning Almighty God. He is the nicest Father, for His mercy endures forever. He is the smartest, for by His wisdom He made the Heavens and the Earth. My Father is the greatest doctor and repairman for the Bible calls Him, Jehovah Raphe, The God That Healeth. He is the greatest boss, for He is El Elyon, Hebrew for the Most High God. God above all gods. Name above all names! My Father Can Do Anything!!! Nothing is too hard for Him!! And with Him all things are possible!!

    Let me tell you what He does for me. My Father gives me everything. My desire is to please Him; therefore, He gives me all the desires of my heart. For He is Jehovah Jireh, the Lord That Provides. My Father not only makes me feel better when others are mean to me, but He makes it right! He prepares a table before me in the presence of my enemies. My Father not only makes me happy, but He gives me joy and peace that most people cannot understand, for He is Jehovah Shalom, the Lord Of Peace. He takes me to places I have never dreamed of. He leads me down paths of righteousness, to still waters, to green pastures for He is Jehovah Raah, the Lord Is My Shepherd, and in Him I want for nothing. He is the greatest teacher because He grants wisdom, generously to all those who ask. And He is **not** a "weekend father," or a "Sunday Dad," or an "absent father." For He is Jehovah Shammah, the Lord That Is There, and He will never, *never*, **ever**, **ever**, leave or forsake me!! And I am an heir to the throne of God. Joined with Christ my King and my brother. I feel like one of those young children and I want to tell everyone who my Daddy is, and what He has done, and what He can do. I am an heir to greatness, to success, to a destiny filled with promise; and may my face always show that **He truly is the greatest in the whole wide world!!**

But....not everyone shares my Father. There is another group, a larger group. Their father is the father of darkness. The father of lies. The father of sin and all that God hates. Theirs is the father of death and destruction. The father of hate. The father of loneliness. The father of anger and sickness and disease. For that father is Satan himself. The devil. The prince of darkness. No matter what name he goes by, he is still a thief and he comes **only** to steal, to kill, and to destroy. So they too, like that other group, live with violence, anger, death, and abandonment. They are heirs to death, destruction, and to hell.

But all thanks be to God Almighty because that group does not have to stay there. Unlike those small children who don't have a choice as to who their father is....we do!! As we have discussed throughout the other chapters, we all are children in the eyes of God and we fall into one of two groups. There are no others! He also says that we can not be a member of both groups. We can not sit on the fence our whole lives and hope that we did enough good so that when we die, we fall onto the heavenly side. Jesus plainly, clearly, absolutely said that everyone must make a conscious choice. Either one side or the other. Either the first group, the enthusiastic group, the ones covered with protection, promise, and love. Or the second group, the ones outside the circle, the ones experiencing distress, abandonment, and destruction. Joshua 24:14 says, "choose this day whom you will serve," So...I guess my question is....Who's your Daddy?"

Let's Go Over It Again!
Chapter Nineteen

When I have just taught my children something new, we review it again. Sometimes we review it....again....and again! It's not because they aren't very smart; it's because our minds need time to adapt to a new way of thinking. The Bible tells us, in Romans 12:2 (paraphrased), not to conform to the ways of this world, but to be transformed by the renewing of our minds. We need to take time to study, understand, and accept change in our lives. In order to make something a part of who we are, we need to make the time, and the effort, to adapt. The scriptures tell us to be careful not to let Satan rob us of knowledge and to watch out for the doubt that he tries to plant in our minds. We study the Bible because that is how we learn the nature of God and who He is. We don't study for God's benefit. He already knows what's in the Bible. We study for our benefit. So we don't waste precious time on this earth, living in confusion and defeat.

Two thousand years ago a bunch of self-righteous people, addicted to religion, made a mess of God's law. Some people, obsessed with tradition and control, led the masses into a distorted understanding of God. Sure, there was some truth to almost everything that was taught, but like today, truth can be interpreted and distorted to create new faiths and beliefs.

But God had an answer for His people......Jesus. I can just imagine God looking at his Son and saying, "Go down there, Son, and set everybody straight." So, He came to earth to once again show all of humanity God's mercy and forgiveness. Because Jesus emphasized love, justice, and respect for free will, it blew those religious leaders away. They didn't know what to make of Him as He revealed the root of their problems.....You all put religion before God!!! You all get crazy over-regulating things. They were *really* unhappy with Him when He exposed them as religious control-freaks who represented God, but didn't reflect God. They wanted people to be measured according to their standards, instead of God's standards. Jesus was loved by those who wanted to be free from ridiculous, religious rules, but was hated by those who laid the foundations of church politics and legalism. However, those very bricks of self-righteousness and bondage which they laid, paved their own road to hell.

Today we see a familiar scene with a contemporary twist. We have suicide bombers with no respect for life, that kill unarmed people in the name of religion. We have terrorists that believe they benefit society by killing innocent people because of their religion. We have abusive, spiritual authorities that molest children and trample trusting adults, as they hide behind their status and their religion. We have spiritual leaders in the world that improperly interpret the scriptures, and openly stand for issues that God clearly says He hates. As in Biblical times, we have many self-righteous people, addicted to religion, that misrepresent God and champion a cause for yet one more church denomination.

But God has an answer for His people today…….. Jesus. And He is sending Him again, for the final time. To fulfill His plan of redemption. The message of Jesus that has gone unchanged for two thousand years. Just as He told those poor, misguided people in Biblical times, He's telling us, today….avoid walking in religion, just walk with Me. I am so glad that Jesus does not judge us according to the position of our religion, but according to the position of our hearts.

God wants us to be reasonable with His word. As a new parent, we don't expect a newborn baby to go home, graduate from college, apply for a mortgage, and win the Nobel Peace Prize all in the same day. And God does not expect such unreasonable maturity, either. God intends for us to take it slow. He intends for us to use His scriptures literally, but in a practical way. We know that our children are not born knowledgeable, mature, wise little people ready to blossom into their fullest potential. So, when we are "born again" let's not expect ourselves to immediately be wise and at optimum performance. Somehow, many of us presume that the moment we meet Jesus we instantaneously understand all the ways of God. It's as if the gates of heaven open up and revelation pours down on our heads as God reveals all His secrets. We think we should immediately be annointed with the wisdom of Solomon, the passion of David, and the strength of Samson. We don't think we ought to reveal any weaknesses and we should never feel hurt or afflicted. We should never be wrong; we should always be bold; overflowing with solutions to all problems. We should be strong at all times and be able to do it and know it all. But if that were true, we wouldn't be like God...we would be God.

Remember the woman caught in the act of adultery? Jesus did not condemn her, He just told her to go and sin no more. The key word was **go**. As she went she realized the most important decision of her life. After she met a loving and forgiving Lord, she had to turn around and decide what she was going to do next. She could go back and pick up where she left off, but there would be a small voice in her heart crying out that she was living a lesser life than what God had designed for her. There would always be a whisper in her mind, reminding her that she was living short of her best. **Or** she could embrace that forgiveness and live a life that reflected a new chance to be all that God created her for.

This is the same choice that we are all presented with. It was the same then as it is now. Through the forgiveness of Jesus we are given a choice....this very moment....to go and sin no more. Whether you like it or not, you are now the woman that is at the feet of Jesus. It's just between Him and you. All your sin is exposed; and He is, without condemnation, giving you that very same choice. Go and sin no more. When you are done reading this book some of you will try to forget what you have read. You can go back, and pick up where you left off, but there will be a small voice in your heart whispering that you are living a lesser life than what God had designed for you. You, too, will hear an occasional faint cry reminding you that you are living short of your best. **Or** you can embrace that forgiveness and live a life that reflects a new chance to be all that God created you to be. Just as she did, you will go, and you will make your choice.

Although God certainly wants us to choose Him, He gives us free will. If you choose to walk away and not accept God's gift, it may be difficult to forget the love and compassion of Jesus. The fact that He is **not** standing there ready to throw a stone at you, will be replayed in the memory of your heart. Situations will present themselves that may cause you to question your decision….because you know that way down deep inside you…that whisper you keep hearing in your soul….is God himself. That same nagging and tugging at your heart is the same voice that has changed the minds of many skeptics. What everyone must understand, however, is that once you die, it will be too late to change your mind. The Bible is clear that there will be no acceptable excuse. And if the Lord returns for His Church before you have made that decision, it will also be too late. Then all that will be left is regret and blame as people hold God responsible for sending them to hell. The truth is, God does not send anyone to hell; we make our own choice where we wish to spend eternity.

I used to think when I heard the term "repent" that it meant one had to fall on their face as if one was auditioning for a role in "The Exorcist!" Dramatic sobbing and howling, followed by anguishing proclamations of what wretched sinful, spawns of hell we were. No wonder people think twice.....it looks painful. We don't have to scream toward heaven. God's not deaf. Repent simply means to be sorry and then to change. Just being sorry without changing or changing without being sorry, is incomplete. We need forgiveness **and** change for salvation.

If you're anything like me, change can be an exciting thing, but it can also be an uncomfortable thing. I usually embrace the "idea" of change, but don't want anything to do with the process. I have to remind myself that I am a child of God and when He wants something from me, or wants me to do something, I can trust that my life will always improve. He wants me to put my problems and my questions in His one hand, and then He will open the other hand and offer me the answers.

I don't believe that there is a magic formula or a certain poem that one can say to invite Jesus into their lives. Only some heartfelt words, a prayer, asking Him for forgiveness, and recognizing that we need him for eternal life. Just Him, not religion. John 3:36 says, "Whoever believes in the Son has eternal life, but whoever rejects the Son will not see life, for God's wrath remains on him." Acts 4:12 says, "Salvation is found in no one else, for there is no other name under heaven given to men by which we must be saved." Ephesians 2:8-9, "For it is by grace you have been saved, through faith--and this not from yourselves, it is the gift of God--not by works, so that no one can boast." God's grace offers us salvation. There is nothing we can do to earn it.

The Bible says that when you believe, you are made

new. That doesn't mean that you will wake up tomorrow being your neighbor. It means how God sees you is new. He has taken the old you, the old sin, and removed it forever. 2 Corinthians 5:17 says, "Therefore, if anyone is in Christ, he is a new creation; the old has gone, the new has come!" He no longer sees us as the sinner or as the heathen.

Even if you have prayed and still don't feel saved, it doesn't matter....you still are. That's a trick of Satan, to make us feel like we are too bad to ever receive redemption; our sins are too many for God's forgiveness. He tells us that if we don't feel saved, then we must not be saved. Again, he's just playing on our emotions. We all know he's a liar. Upon repentance, Jesus wipes away all sin, never to be remembered again. Psalm 103:12-13 says, "as far as the east is from the west, so far has he removed our transgressions from us. As a father has compassion on his children, so the Lord has compassion on those who fear him;" To fear God is to respect God.

You see, forgiveness is not about deserving, it's about accepting. What has changed is our standing with God. Because Jesus covers us with His perfection, God only sees perfection, flawlessness, and righteousness! Another trick of Satan is to plant a seed of skepticism in people's hearts. If you are a doubter, that seed was probably planted some time ago. He wants you to believe that any good person can get to heaven, because he knows that if you believe that, you won't ever get there.

It is very important to find a Bible-based church, led by God. Not an opinion-based church. If you find a church that has all the answers, then the truth is they probably don't have any. The church must point to God for He is the only one with all the answers. Remember, churches aren't filled entirely with hypocrites, some are trying hard and others have just been grounded for a long time.

There are no perfect people, so there is no perfect church. Don't look for a perfect church, just look for one that's trying hard! Remember, God is not looking at the religious position that we may hold, He's looking at the position of our hearts. Surround yourself with godliness. Christian radio, Christian TV, Christian friends and when you come across some questionable teachings (and you will) find the answers. Remember, God promises to give wisdom to all who ask. He might just be looking at you, to set a few things straight with others.

Two of the most life changing verses in the Bible is James 4:7 and 8, "Submit yourselves, then, to God. Resist the devil, and he will flee from you. Come near to God and he will come near to you." Meaning kick Satan out and move Jesus in. Kick skepticism and condemnation out and invite forgiveness and freedom in. With these verses I get to embrace freedom. God liberates His people from everything that is negative. I get to walk in victory everyday. I am able to live a life of excellence. I am given the ability to throw out fear and permanently invite peace in. He died for me so that I could live freely and blessedly through Him. He shed His blood so my life could be lived to the fullest and I don't intend to waste a single drop of it. He conquered death to show us how valuable we are, each one of us, and to show us that God's promises are still valid, even today. Jeremiah 29:11 says, "For I know the plans I have for you, declares the Lord, plans to prosper you and not to harm you, plans to give you hope and a future."

If you already know the Lord, I pray that you have, at the very least, been encouraged to walk on higher ground with a strengthened heart, renewed spirit, and a renewed passion for living with God. Because everyone perceives God a little bit differently, I pray that everyone will understand God as the loving, compassionate, fair Father that He is. That all will see that He is a big God that does really big things. I pray that you will be encouraged to live without wondering **if** God is going to show up, but live in confidence that He **will** show up! Even if you have known the Lord for a long time, I pray that you are encouraged to commit all you have to Him, so you can live larger, dream bigger, and love Him more deeply.

If you are still breathing, then it's not too late to ask Jesus to forgive you and for you to forgive yourself. No matter what you may think, or how you may feel, God has not forgotten you. He has not left you. He is waiting for you!

I remember, like it was yesterday, that following the agony of childbirth, there was an unspeakable joy. When I looked into those eyes, I knew it was all worth it. Through my tears, I looked at my baby and said, "I'm glad you finally decided to arrive....I've been waiting for you!"

Jesus remembers, like it was yesterday, that following the agony of the cross, there was an unspeakable joy. When He looks into our eyes, He knows it was all worth it! Through His tears, He looks at us and says, "I'm glad you finally decided to arrive....I've been waiting for you!"

God, What Exactly Do You Want From Me?

Chapter Twenty

Just be my child.